14.95

Dogwatch and Liberty Days

Dogwatch and Liberty Days

Seafaring Life in the Nineteenth Century

MARGARET S. CREIGHTON

THE PEABODY MUSEUM OF SALEM

*Dogwatch and Liberty Days: Seafaring Life in the
Nineteenth Century* was published in conjunction with
an exhibition of the same name which opened at the
Peabody Museum of Salem on October 2, 1982. The
exhibition and the catalogue were made possible by a
generous grant from the National Endowment for the
Humanities.

Cover illustration (color) by Thomas Davidson, Salem,
Massachusetts, 1854, Peabody Museum, Salem.

Library of Congress Catalogue
Card No. G540.C73 1982

ISBN 0-87577-071-1 hardcover
ISBN 0-87577-070-3 paperback

Designed by David Ford
Typeset by DEKR Corporation
Printed by Mercantile Press, Worcester, Massachusetts.

Manufactured in the United States of America

Contents

Acknowledgments

Dogwatch and Liberty Days was developed and produced through the kindness and assistance of a number of institutions and individuals. The Peabody Museum of Salem, with help from the National Endowment for the Humanities, was the prime mover behind the project, and I am grateful to its director, Peter Fetchko, for his long-standing support. I also appreciate the help of Barbara Edkins, librarian, Paul Johnston, curator of maritime history, Paul Winfisky, keeper of pictures, and Markham Sexton and his colleagues in the Photography Department. My deepest thanks, too, to Sheila Hones, my project associate. Without her good humor and intelligence, her calm patience and perseverance, this project, composed of so many disparate elements, would never have managed to become a coherent whole.

For their untiring help with my library research I thank the following: Ellen Mark, Irene Norton, and Caroline Preston of The Essex Institute, Salem, Massachusetts; Barbara Johnson, of Princeton, New Jersey; Robert Ellis, Stuart Frank, Kenneth Martin, and John Sheldon of the Kendall Whaling Museum, Sharon, Massachusetts; Anne Goodrich of the Blunt White Library, Mystic, Connecticut; Paul Cyr of the New Bedford Free Public Library, New Bedford, Massachusetts; Virginia Adams and Philip Purrington of the Old Dartmouth Historical Society, New Bedford, Massachusetts; Edouard Stackpole of the Peter Foulger Museum, Nantucket, Massachusetts; Susan Glover Godlewski of the Providence Public Library, Providence, Rhode Island.

For their helpful scholarly criticism I am obliged to two historians: James A. Henretta of Boston University and Benjamin W. Labaree of Mystic Seaport and Williams College.

For her generous hospitality and her gracious good humor I extend my most profound thanks to Mrs. George Kellom, whose grandfather, Isaac Baker, wrote so many journals at sea with such skill and such wit that he could have inspired this entire project on his own.

And, finally, for their personal as well as their professional support, my wholehearted appreciation goes to J. S. Borthwick, Susan Ransom, Nancy Gurney, Susan Gurney, and to my husband, Rob Smith.

Author's Note

Maritime and social historians who want to study aspects of seafaring life from primary sources are fortunate that sailors left behind so many written records. Every vessel that sailed in the nineteenth century carried a log keeper, usually the first mate, who maintained a regular account of the weather, sail changes, and his ship's position. Besides this official log keeper, there were other note-taking seamen. Some sailors kept records of their voyages that were, in their terseness and technical detail, almost identical to formal logs. Others combined their reports of shipboard life with introspection and personal narration, and it is these manuscripts, labelled journals or diaries, that form the basis of *Dogwatch and Liberty Days*.

Both logs and journals are stored, sometimes by the hundreds, in maritime museums, public libraries, and historical societies. Among them are some that are illustrated with small watercolor paintings, and pen or pencil drawings. Each of these illustrated manuscripts is an extraordinary find, and is well-worthy of publication in its own right. Seen together, as many of these illustrations are here, they offer the public a visual perspective on seafaring that it has rarely enjoyed.

The text of *Dogwatch and Liberty Days* does not include footnotes. Scholars and other researchers should be able to identify each primary source cited, however, by means of the list of journal keepers placed toward the end of this volume. Similarly, catalogue information about illustrations and objects is contained in the rear. All objects, except where noted otherwise, are part of the permanent collection of the Peabody Museum of Salem. Sources of illustrations are noted by each photograph.

Sailors' language is sometimes idiosyncratic in its syntax, grammar, and spelling. Since it has been transcribed from original manuscripts verbatim, a word or letter has occasionally been inserted within square brackets to avoid confusion.

Introduction

As everyone familiar with the sea must know, and as sailors repeatedly confirm, life aboard a ship in the nineteenth century was rigorous and demanding. Mariners, especially those on long deepwater sailing voyages, faced enormous physical and emotional hardships. In their journals, sailors describe the punishments of their profession in remarkable detail. But at the same time they tell us that seafaring offered something besides pain and toil. They speak of hours in the early evening at sea, during the dogwatch, when they sang and danced with their shipmates. They describe days of sublime sunsets, exhilarating winds, and, even for the veteran sailor, fresh discoveries. And they tell, too, of liberty days, when their pent up energies and stored frustrations were released in a sudden jubilant spree on shore.

This account of seafaring acknowledges the well-known difficulties of ocean life, but in addition gives special consideration to its numerous and varied delights.

Dogwatch and Liberty Days has been made possible by the work of sailors themselves. Its text is drawn from the journals of 104 seafaring men, it is illustrated by photographs of journal sketches and paintings, and it is supplemented by photographs of objects used or manufactured on shipboard. To a large extent, then, this account of seafaring in nineteenth-century America is an insiders' story, told not by those who viewed deep water from safe harbors, but by mariners who experienced all the pains and pleasures a voyage could produce.

In the mid-1800s, at the height of America's sailing enterprise, over 100,000 seamen left the United States annually for foreign destinations, according to reports of the federal treasury. Among the men who set out in American sailing ships between 1830 and 1875 were some who decided that it was worth their time and energy to keep a diary of their voyages, and it is the efforts of one hundred and four of these men that inform this account. While these sailors represent a sizable number of witnesses, they may not speak for all mariners, and it is important to understand who they were in order to appreciate their particular angles of vision.

At the time they wrote these journals, all of these men were deepwater sailors. Their ships crossed the equator in search of either whales or foreign cargo on voyages lasting one to four years. Not one of their diaries records the events of a naval cruise, a coastal voyage, or a transatlantic crossing, and even though the exigencies of whaling and trading meant that some would enter the Arctic Ocean or stop in European ports, most of their journals are dominated by experiences in the southern hemisphere.

These seafaring journal keepers, seventy-six whalemen and twenty-eight merchant seamen, represent all levels of a ship's hierarchy. Of those whose positions are known, forty-three were officers, eleven were cooks and stewards, fourteen were boatsteerers and coopers, and forty were foremast hands and cabin boys. Even though the emphasis in *Dogwatch and Liberty Days* is on life in the forecastle, diarists of all ranks have been called on to provide a variety of perspectives.

In demographic terms, these hundred-odd journal keepers were remarkably alike. All except one were white. All were American, and most had hometowns on or near the northeast coast. Most were young men. The average age of the twenty-six non-officers who listed their ages was twenty-two when they began the voyages they describe.

To what extent were these men typical of other American deepwater sailors? Nineteenth-century crew lists from the ports of Salem, New York City, and New Bedford, examined at random, suggest that the majority of men sailing from these ports in the mid-1800s were young, were from coastal regions, and, except for stewards and cooks, were white.* These lists do not, of course, indicate a sailor's economic or social class, his degree of literacy, or his education, and thus it is difficult to determine the representativeness of the diarists in these significant areas. Obviously, all of these sailors could write English, and, given such a capacity, they may not have spoken for seamen who did not possess such skills, and whose beliefs and behavior may have differed from their own.

It is important to recognize that *Dogwatch and Liberty Days* presents a view of seafaring that may be biased by a culture, class, or race. In many ways its perspective may be a broad one—the testimony of over one hundred sailors deserves serious credit—but as one mariner named Richard Boyenton remarked in 1834, sailors were "a hetregenious mass of incongruity," and this fact should not be forgotten.

---

* These lists, however, must be examined with some caution. Because American vessels in the mid-nineteenth century were required by law to carry crews that were two-thirds American, there was a strong motive for shipmasters, agents, and customs officials to falsify lists so that foreign seamen could be shipped. How many crew lists contain false information with regard to sailors' nationalities is unknown. Even if crew lists were 100 percent accurate, it should be noted that they only describe the crew which left or entered American ports. During the course of a voyage the nationality of a crew might change several times.

Oilskin Pants

Oil-soaked pants like these were vital to sailors who worked in drenching rains. In wet weather, sailors wore waterproofed hats, pants, and jackets, but often went barefoot so they would not slip on rigging as they climbed aloft.

Edward Haskell, *Tarquin,* 1862
Peabody Museum of Salem

Tuesda[y] ... Weather pleasa[nt] ... noon, but first ... a fine breeze sh[ip] ... Indications of ba[d] ... Abou[t] ... com[m] ... hard. ... were c[...]

YANKEY TAR

Sailors throughout the world were known as "tars," no doubt because they made liberal use of tar to water-proof and preserve clothes and ships' rigging. For some seamen, a "sea tan," created by a combination of sun exposure and tar stain, was a sign of prestige that they looked forward to showing off on shore.

Anonymous Sketchbook, n.d.

Kendall Whaling Museum

Tarred Hat

One of the few articles of sailors' clothing that has survived from the nineteenth century is this straw hat covered with tar. Most garments were in such sorry shape by the end of voyage, and had been patched so often, that they were probably incinerated as soon as a seaman reached home.

Sea Chest with Belongings

A sea chest was probably the most versatile object a sailor owned. It was his table, his chair, his bureau, and, in the worst of times, his bed. In addition, the sea chest served a social function. It provided entertainment for the mariner who was at a loss for employment or pleasure and who could, in his spare moments, "overhaul" his chest, move shirts to the left, tobacco to the top, pants to the middle, and then repeat the process over and over again. "One that never was on a long voyage may think this foolishness," wrote a sailor named Horace Putnam in the 1850s, "but they know little how dull times are sometimes."

Like "tar," "Jack" was a universal and generic title for a sailor. As one foremast hand named Horace Putnam explained, "Jack is what we always call a sailor when we don't know his real name."

George Soule, *St. George*, 1865–69

Nicholson Whaling Collection

86 Days out.

Ship George from Salem towards Calcutta

H.	K.	H.K.	Courses.	Winds.	Lee.	Remarks. Thursday Nov. 23
1	8		S. by E. ½ E.			
2	8			S. E.		
3	8					
4	8					
5	8					
6	8					
7	8					
8	8					Continued the same, as yesterday's
9	8	1				
10	8	1				
11	8			South		
12	8					
1	8					
2	8					
3	8					
4	8					
5	7					
6	7	1				
7	7	1		S. S. E.		
8	7	1				
9	7					
10	7					Long. by Chron. 85° 52' East
11	7					
12	7					

Course.	Dist.	Diff. lat.	Dep.	Lat. by D. R.	Lat. by Ob.	Varia.	Diff. Long.	Long. in.	Long. by Ob.
S. 11° E.	187	3° 3' S.	36' E.	16° 13' S.	16° 20' S.	5° W.	38' E.	81° 55' East	

On the "Look-out"

Even though most sailors used the terms "log" and "journal" interchangeably, historians distinguish between the two types of voyage accounts. A terse, business-like account, like that of the ship *George*, above, is considered a log, while the personal account of the *Tarquin*, below, is labelled a journal, in this case an illustrated one.

Andrew Haraden, *George*, 1831
Edward Haskell, *Tarquin*, 1862

Peabody Museum of Salem

1
Rude Awakenings

I sailed but as the last hill went beneath the horison I found instead of contentment that I was the most unhappy mortal liveing.

—Ambrose Bates on the bark *Milwood*, June 1867

Sailors found some pleasures in seafaring, but rarely during the first week aboard ship. Even before they lost sight of familiar land, in fact, most men began to suffer pains of dislocation. Down in the dark forecastle or up on the swaying deck, young sailors who had never left home before were initiated quickly into the rigors of shipboard life. Although they did their best to fend off nausea as they stumbled through their first jobs, most succumbed to seasickness almost immediately, and the scene recorded by the cooper on the ship *Congress* on New Year's Day, 1857, was a universal one: "Finding every thing in readiness, we put out with a fair wind, and amused ourselves by watching the 'green hands' as they tried to walk decks, first pitching to one side, then to the other, and soon those disagreeable emotions of the stomach were visibly haunting them, as they would jump to the side and heave."

Those crew members who were off duty below decks were no better off, for they endured the horrors of a suffocating, smelly forecastle whose very air acted as an emetic. After his first day at sea in October 1858, seaman William Abbe described a situation that was shared by nearly every foremast hand: "I was so fatigued that I turned in early—but the novelty of my situation—and the un-comfortable air of the forecastle—increased by the breath of sixteen men . . . [and the] stench of the vomit from the sick men—prevented me from sleeping much." The

men were so sick on Abbe's ship, in fact, that they did not have the will to clean the deck of the small living quarters, which collected a compound of "bits of meat and bread—onion skins—spilt coffee—tobacco spittle."

Even though they were repeatedly sick, greenhands, as inexperienced sailors were called, were ordered at once to perform duties, to take in sail, to haul on lines, and to break out supplies and food. Their inability to understand the commands of officers amused the experienced crew, who, while they might have come aboard drunk, at least comported themselves with self-confidence. Greenhands were the objects of endless teasing about their "landlubberliness." The old hands on the whaleship *Sunbeam* in 1868, for example, chose as their target one neophyte named Smith who not only had trouble tying a square knot but had the misfortune of referring to ropes and lines as "strings." To make matters worse, he fell into fits of crying on the subject of his elderly grandmother, which elicited gleeful and eager jeers from his shipmates.

New sailors like Smith not only struggled with the physical trials of seafaring but also gained some disturbing insights into human behavior. They learned quickly that most private property was not respected at sea and that their belongings were to be shared. Young William Townsend discovered this soon after leaving on a voyage from Massachusetts to the Orient in 1858. He had sailed with carefully packed tins and boxes of fruit and sweets to help temper the monotony of ship fare. No sooner had Townsend left his bunk to attend to his duties as a cabin boy, however, than the men belonging to the first mate's watch broke into his plum cakes and gingerbread. "To[o] mean it is," wrote Townsend in a state of dejection, ". . . its hard work this going to sea." There was hardly a green sailor who did not share Townsend's misery after a week on shipboard, and many vowed to leave their vessels at the first opportunity. Others expressed the sentiments of young John Battis, who, after looking forward to seafaring life, found himself sadly disillusioned by the actual experience. As he noted in his diary six days after leaving Boston in 1864:

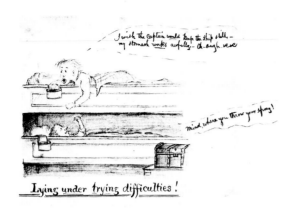

Isaac Baker, *Merrimac,* 1858
Private Collection

"Oh dear I'm *so* sick," inscribed Isaac Baker beneath this illustration. "Will somebody throw me overboard?"

Isaac Baker, *Merrimac,* 1858
Private Collection

Monday October 24 the day was stormy I wish I were at home of all the places on earth there is no place like home I wanted to go to sea and now I have got enough of it Sunday I laid in my Bunk and cried. . . .

In the aftercabin, shipmasters and mates were equally cheerless. While they were not afflicted with seasickness, many experienced severe depression over leaving their friends and families. "Oh God! my wife. Talk about dieing. I hope that I shal never suffer any keener pangs than those that now pierce my heart," wrote Captain Samuel Braley of the *Arab* in 1849. Mate Edward Jenney echoed these sentiments in 1859: "The Lord only knows my feelings. What shall I do. My little children. I wish I had never been born."

Those men who did not feel as if they were dying from the pain of separation suffered from a fear that they might never return home at all. This fear was not, of course, a paranoid obsession, but an anxiety based on a sad truth of seafaring. Sailors' journals suggest that nearly every vessel on a long deepwater voyage suffered the death of at least one sailor aboard ship and one or two others in foreign ports. What frightened experienced sailors, however, was less the chance of dying than the probably violent, isolated nature of that death. Most mariners who died at sea did not pass away quietly in the company of friends. Many fell from aloft in rough weather, either crashing onto hard decks or falling into the cold, turbulent water of a desolate ocean. Others went much more slowly, dying of infections such as malaria, dysentery, or venereal diseases, all easily contracted in foreign ports. Each seafaring trade had special dangers. A whaleman risked death every time he stepped into a whaleboat to pursue his prey. He could be flung out of a boat and dragged under water by the spinning line that was attached to the whale, thrust into the air by its flukes, or separated with his fellow whalemen from the mother ship—to perish in the dark or the fog.

Besides the diseases and accidents that threatened individual whalemen, there were dangers that could destroy an entire ship's company. Whalers regularly wandered into treacherous waters. Some sailed into the western Arctic Ocean to look for bowhead whales, and those that lingered there were in serious danger of being crushed by ice. Ships on the Pacific Ocean had to beware of uncharted reefs and islands, where they might run aground at night and be broken up by pounding waves before rescue was possible.

Merchant vessels had their own problems. Their eagerness to reach port meant that they had to take advantage of every available wind, and their small crews worked hard and fast to change sails at every fluctuation in the weather. Losing a man overboard from a yardarm in a squall or gale was all too common an event on a cargo ship. Merchantmen also ran the risk of being hit and sunk by another vessel at night. Unlike whalemen, who often worked in little-traveled waters, merchantmen sailed shipping routes with other trading vessels, all of whom crowded on sail in a strong wind. While the chance that one ship might rush headlong into another was remote, it still happened, as those who had narrowly escaped such disaster reported. Horace Putnam, a seaman on the *William Schroder* of Salem in the 1840s, experienced such a near miss in the middle of a spring night in the Atlantic Ocean. A large ship, "with studding sails low and aloft," and which looked, Putnam said, like the "Phantom Ship of olden story," rushed by them in the dark, narrowly missing their vessel. "All that was said or thought of it," wrote Putnam, "was that David Jones did not get us this time, though we are consigned to his locker one of these days."

The full horrors of perishing at sea were expressed by a steward named Charles Benson on the bark *Glide* on the night of May 22, 1862. After he had fallen asleep in the cabin, Benson was "awakened by lowed talk on deck. it was caused by the larbard watch hearing something to leward which sounded like some one haloing in destress. they heared it 3 times. but it was dark & it blew half a gale. they could not tell for certain but the mate says he thinks it was someone clinging to something in the water. it has made me feal sad."

The ordeals of seafaring were not restricted, of course, to homesickness, physical danger, and the fear of death. Sailors also had to face the considerable discomforts and deprivations of

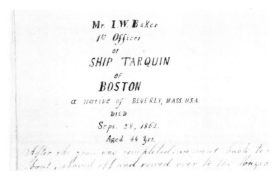

On September 28, 1862, Isaac Baker, whose drawings and writings appear here in large numbers, died after succumbing to a tropical disease in Sumatra. By coincidence, one of Baker's shipmates, Edward Haskell, also illustrated and maintained a journal, and Baker's last days, from the beginning of his fever on September 18, to the hour he "breathed his last," were noted with affectionate detail.

Edward Haskell, *Tarquin,* 1862
Peabody Museum of Salem

Edward Haskell and three of his shipmates buried their first mate, Isaac Baker, at Rigas, in Sumatra. After rowing the coffin ashore seven miles from their ship, the sailors carried it "slowly" on two oars to a grave they had dug under some coconut trees. The second mate then read a prayer, after which the coffin was lowered into the earth.

Edward Haskell, *Tarquin,,* 1862
Peabody Museum of Salem

The bark *LaGrange* encountered severe weather and heavy seas as she rounded Cape Horn in early June, 1849. On June first, the winds were so strong that the ship was forced to "lay to under bare poles," because the wind would have ripped even the smallest sail to shreds. At least one of the *LaGrange*'s sailors began to fear for his life. "If we don't have a change soon," wrote journal-keeper Henry Tuttle, "we shall begin to think about Davy Jones." Fortunately, the winds abated, and the bark made its way safely into the Pacific Ocean. Tuttle demonstrates the precariousness of a sailor's job with his sketch of the man aloft on the royal yard furling a sail in the storm.

Henry Tuttle, *LaGrange*, 1849
Essex Institute

Edward Haskell, *Tarquin*, 1862
Peabody Museum of Salem

everyday shipboard life. The food they were served was often unpalatable and always monotonous. Meals usually consisted of four staples—salt meat, hard bread, rice, and beans. This menu was supplemented no more than twice a week by a serving of duff, a boiled flour pudding occasionally made with raisins.

Even if sailors found no grounds for complaint in the tedium of their meals, they always had something to say about the condition of their food: the duff was burned, the bread was sour, the water smelled, the pork was rusty, the beef was foul, and everything was infested with insects. It was on the subject of their "grub," in fact, that sailors waxed most eloquent, and nearly every one of these diarists described his food with graphic detail. John Cleland on the ship *Ceres* noted, for example, that the butter that his captain sent forward to the crew on September 23, 1836, was "so strong that if a cockroach comes near it turns him fin out." Horace Putnam, a seaman on the merchant ship *La Plata* in 1848, claimed that his meals consisted of "stuff they call coffee made by pouring water on the grouns that are left from the master table . . . and buscuits that would make good protection for house roofs instead of slates that is commonly used, being much harder and consequently more durible."

On the whaler *Atkins Adams*, foremast hand William Abbe was confronted with molasses two to three inches deep in cockroaches and water that was "muddy, foul-stinking and warm." At one point on his voyage, Abbe found his food so inedible that he abstained from eating altogether:

our duff this noon heavy & watery was literally filled with dirt & cockroaches—I didn't Eat a morsal of the filthy food—but sat laughing at the discoveries the fellows made as they carefully sliced their duff. "Hallo! heres a piece of old Thompsons hat" cried Johnny—"Heres a big worm"—"look at these cockroaches" "I've bit a cockroach in two"—"lets make Thompson eat 'em when he comes below" came from different Empty mouths.

When they could, sailors took advantage of the marine environment to find meat and brought aboard fish, birds, or porpoise to eat. Whalers occasionally stopped at remote islands

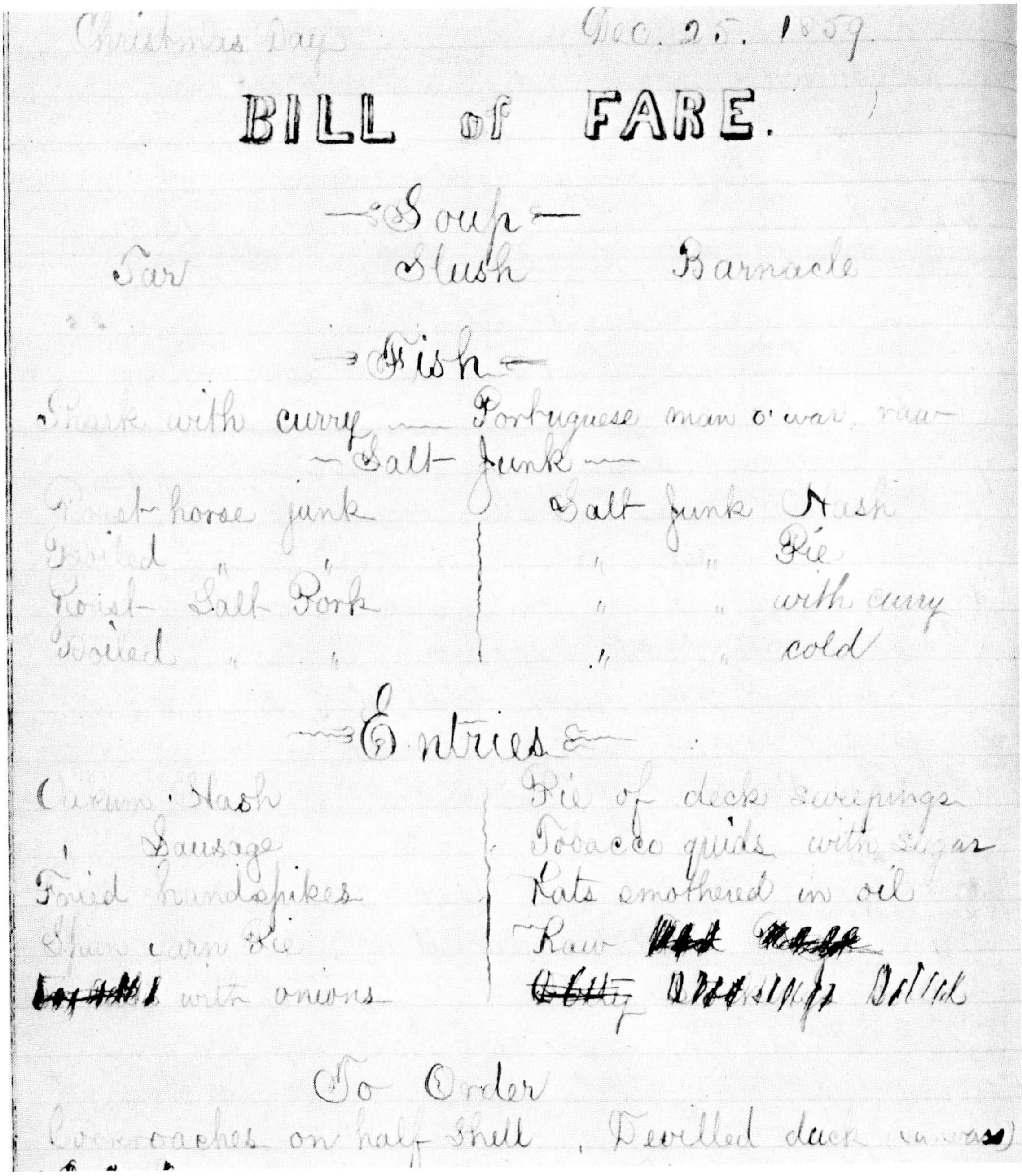

Christmas Day   Dec. 25. 1859.

BILL of FARE.

— Soup —

Tar   Slush   Barnacle

— Fish —

Shark with curry — Portuguese man o'war, raw —

— Salt Junk —

Roast horse junk   Salt Junk Hash
Boiled   "   "   Pie
Roast Salt Pork   "   "   with curry
Boiled   "   "   "   "   cold

— Entries —

Curbans Hash   Pie of deck sweepings
      "   Sausage   Tobacco quids with sugar
Fried handspikes   Rats smothered in oil
Shin corn Pie   Raw ~~bed bugs~~
~~Boiled~~ with onions   ~~Boiled~~ ~~dirty stockings~~

To Order

Cockroaches on half Shell , Devilled duck (in vain)

Unfortunately, Freeman Pulsifer's satiric menu comes
very close to an actual account of ship food. The en-
trees which have been deleted here include raw bed
bugs and boiled dirty stockings.

Freeman Pulsifer, *Reliance,* 1859

Peabody Museum of Salem

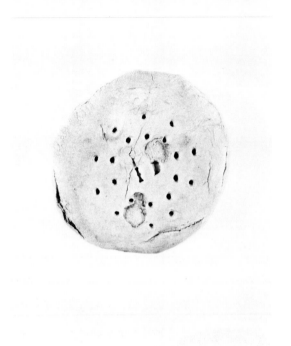

The fact that this biscuit has survived intact for at least a century and a half testifies to its almost inedible hardness. "Soft tack" was a rare treat for sailors before the mast in the mid-nineteenth century, and most men ate hard ship's biscuits like these, occasionally flavored with worms or cockroaches. This particular biscuit was given to the Peabody Museum along with a legend: a young man bound on a voyage to the East Indies in the early 1800s threw this piece of hard bread to his fiancée on the dock, shouting to her that it would be served at their wedding breakfast. She kept the biscuit, waited faithfully for her betrothed, but never heard from the ship or the sailor again.

to restock and to pick up fruit, onions, cabbages, livestock, or whatever they most needed. The food sailors found on remote shores, however, was sometimes no improvement over the food they carried. Edwin Pulver, for instance, discovered that he would prefer almost *anything* to polar bear. It was so strong, he said, that "the devill could Not Eat it," and to commemorate the horrors of the occasion, in August 1852, he offered the readers of his diary the following poem:

I hope when we get more fresh meat
It'll be of A kind that we can eat
I care Not weather it be cow or hog
Nor would I run from A well cooked dog

So here I vow likewise declare
I Ne'r will Eat more polar bear
And if I find it on my plate
I will throw it at the stewarts pate.

Deepwater vessels sometimes carried livestock, usually chickens and pigs, to provide sailors with an occasional fresh mess. A difficulty arose when these animals had to be slaughtered, however, because, as much as seamen wanted fresh meat, they were loath to lose an animal who had become a companion and shipboard pet. Isaac Baker illustrates the sad death, or murder, of Marietta Sow aboard the ship *Warsaw*.

Isaac Baker, *Warsaw*, 1840

Private Collection

Medicine Chest

All nineteenth century vessels of 150 tons or more were required to carry a medicine chest. Shipmasters, or whoever else aboard professed to have some medical knowledge, made liberal use of cures like bleeding, purging, poultices, and emetics. Most used an instruction book to arrive at their diagnoses and treatments.

As one might expect, a constant diet of salt provisions undermined the health of deepwater sailors. Even though most seamen knew that certain fruits and vegetables could prevent and cure vitamin deficiency diseases, it was rarely possible for them to keep fresh produce in stock. Thus malnutrition was a common shipboard condition, and men like J. E. Haviland, who broke both front teeth off "close to the gums" on a piece of hard bread in March 1858, lay in their vessels in sickened states until they either died, were discharged, or received proper food.

Besides facing problems of nutrition, sailors had trouble satisfying other needs. Keeping clean at sea was a formidable challenge, not only because water supplies were often limited, but because shipmasters usually allotted only Sun-

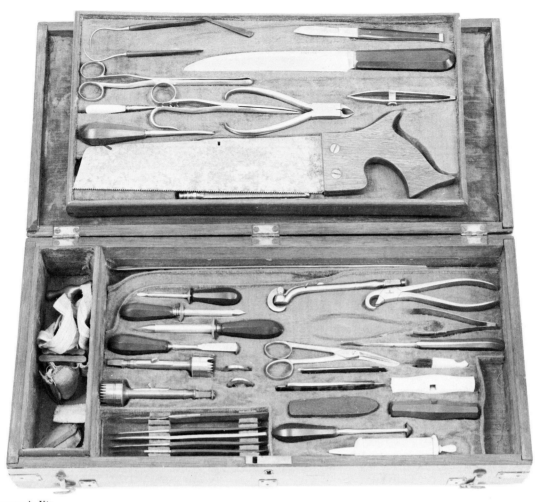

Surgeon's Kit

Sick or injured sailors subjected their bodies to sewing, cutting, and, as this kit indicates, sawing, by shipmasters who worked without anesthesia or professional expertise. Many vessels would not even have carried surgical equipment as sophisticated as this, and sea captains would have had to use tools made for carpentry or sailmaking to perform surgical operations.

days for such an activity. Washing filthy clothes was a particularly odious job for most seamen, and as soon as a sailor could afford to he paid a shipmate to perform the task for him. Those men who did not have extra money struggled to clean clothes with sea water, ashes, or even urine. "I have just begun," wrote greenhand James Allen on the *Alfred Gibbs* in 1870, "to get used to washing in urine and even now some cant wash in it for the smell."

Insufficient sleep was a further hardship of seafaring. Work aboard a sailing ship did not, of course, stop at night, and work shifts, called watches, were organized so that some part of a ship's crew was on duty at all times, to steer, to keep a lookout, and to change sails. On merchant ships, and often on whalers, labor was

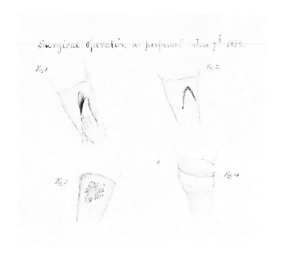

Isaac Baker, *Tarquin,* 1862
Private Collection

divided into a system called "watch and watch," where one half of the crew was on deck for four hours while the other half was off duty. In order to prevent the same sailors from being up at the same time every night, the watch from four to eight in the evening was divided into two short shifts, called "dogwatches." While the etymology of the word dogwatch is unknown, its meaning, to a sailor, was perfectly clear. It was during the dogwatch that sailors were relieved of most of their hard labors, when they took time to eat, spin yarns, or sport together.

When a sailor worked on a "watch and watch" system he rarely, if ever, had a good night's sleep. Even when he was off duty and in his bunk or hammock, the foremast hand in particular was not guaranteed any rest at all. If his shipmates were not playing a loud game of cards or engaging in a fracas of some kind, or up on deck doing a hornpipe over his head, chances were that the tired sailor was battling with the insect world. Nearly every sailor lucky enough to have a mattress also had fleas, cockroaches, or bedbugs. On the *Atkins Adams* cockroaches "actually as large as mice" contested with seamen for forecastle privileges.

Even the aftercabin was not free of crawling and jumping vermin. Mate Isaac Baker on the ship *Warsaw* and steward Silliman Ives on the

Sunbeam were particularly frustrated after they found insects in their bunks. Baker was even possessed enough on April 22, 1841, to carry on a written conversation with a flea just before he killed it. After the flea bit him, Baker entertained the idea of a pardon for the insect but finally decided on retaliation. "Who gave you the liberty," he asked the flea rhetorically, "to commit such bloody depredations on the leg of an American citizen? You plead strongly but revenge is sweet to me as my blood was to you. So Mr. Flea with your leave I will just take the audacious liberty to put a stop to your proceedings.—Now I'm satisfied. If I am convicted of wilful flea slaughter, I must abide the consequences."

Silliman Ives could not take revenge so effectively, for every time he killed one bedbug, another appeared. Their funerals, he wrote on August 9, 1868, are "largely attended. For they always make it a point to show their strength." Ives's frustration with the bugs was compounded by their large numbers and their longevity. "Its mighty hard work to persuade em to leave," he declared.

Ive tried all ways that I ever heard of. Ive tried to come the generous dodge, and give em half my berth, but they are hoggish in their dispositions and choose to root around at their own sweet wills & monopolize the whole. You cant discharge them when you get into port. They are bound to perform the voyage, if not one else does. Politeness availing nothing I've annointed them with kerosine oil, buried em in oil soap, scalded them, pickled em in short done everything that the invention of mortal man could suggest for their extermination, but all to no purpose. They still remain livelier larger and saucier than ever before. Weve got em all sizes, from the bigness of a bung town copper to the minuteness of a small pins head.

Even those sailors who were not plagued by insects and other distractions and who managed to be lulled to sleep by the rush of water or by the creaking of ships' spars were not likely to have uninterrupted rest. "Perhaps," explained Edwin Pulver on the *Columbus* in 1852,

we may close our Eyes in something of a quiet Slumber dreaming of friends and Loved ones on shore prehaps of some fair maden that has promised to be your better half when you return When all of a suden your are roused by the hoarse cry of all hands to save the ship you spring for your life half Naked you find yourself on deck and from there aloft to Secure some sail or prehaps the Ship has sprung a leak you man the pumps but find the water gains on you and Now you know that heaven or hell is soon to be your doom. . . .

Marshall Keith on the bark *Brewster* had similar problems with intrusions into his dreams. Keith, when asleep, had recurrent visions of his girlfriends at home, upon whom he was often making sexual advances. He experienced the rudest of interruptions on January 25, 1864, when the fourth mate walked into his cabin to wake him up. Keith had been having a "high time" with his hands on one Helen Purrington's "Applicobation" when the officer intruded. "If it had not been for him," wrote Keith, "the lord only knows what I would have done to Helen."

Marshall Keith's reveries about hometown girls were, in part, an expression of the social isolation that was, for many sailors, one of the cruelest hardships of seafaring. Even though merchant vessels made faster passages and shorter voyages than whalers, the men in ships of both kinds wrote at length about the problems of sailing shut up in small, solitary worlds. Their preoccupation with mail from America suggests the extent of their loneliness. On the ship *Ann Perry* in 1847, for instance, Ezra Goodnough, who had been lucky enough to receive a letter from a young lady from Salem, sold it promptly to one of his shipmates for "two heads of tobacco, it being a very scarce article."

Even though friends, parents, and wives often duplicated their letters and sent them out by different ships, it was by luck that a piece of correspondence found its way to the appropriate target. Yet sailors continued to hope, and when a vessel pulled into port or spoke another ship at sea, one of the first things seamen sought was the mail. Steward Silliman Ives claimed that of all the people in the world, "a sailor prizes a letter the most." On his vessels the conversations of sailors who were about to go into port all centered around the expectation of letters. "And if it is known," he wrote in 1870, "that Jack, or Ben, or Dick, were paying particular attention to any certain young lady, previous to sailing, or if they are supposed to be engaged to get 'spliced' when the voyage is concluded,

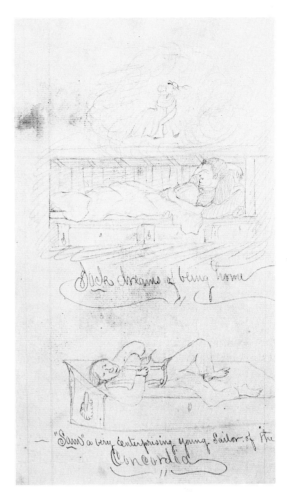

Anonymous, *Concordia,* 1867
Nicholson Whaling Collection

many are the jokes that are cracked at their expense and numerous are the wishes of their messmates, that they may get good long ones, and chock full of love." Ives explained that the very moment his ship came to anchor, a boat went in for the mail and returned as quickly as possible:

Watch the various countenances as the ship's company crowd aft to the quarter deck, where the mate is untying the bundle and looking over the contents. Notice how eagerly they listen as he calls the names of the fortunate ones. One fellow carries off two, another three, or four, or perhaps five. Some get only one but they think that they are lucky to get that, while many who have been anxiously waiting, and were 'sure they should get one anyhow,' turn sadly

Mail Bag

The system of mail delivery at sea was haphazard at best, but one of the surest ways of sending a letter back to America was to waylay a homeward bound vessel, and to send a bag full of mail over to her to take home. Even those sailors who could not write added to the mail bag, for they dictated their messages to literate shipmates.

away as the last name is called, hardly able to repress a tear at their bitter disappointment.

The mail, of course, did not always bring the best tidings. Often it carried news that only increased a sailor's frustration and loneliness. When young Charles Barnard reached port on the *Resolute* in 1859, he heard of the death of his young sister, aged four. "This is the life of a sailor," he wrote, "to hear the tidings of home and . . . not be there to see her before she was buried." Other seamen learned of sicknesses or of possible engagements in their hometowns and knew that they were powerless to affect any change in the faraway events. Captain Samuel Braley, for one, experienced fits of agitation during the time his wife expected to deliver their child, but knew that he would have to wait seven months before he had any word of the birth. On the first of April, 1850, he glumly noted the following in his diary: "I am now a husband and father of the dead or the living; and I would give much to know which; but I shant till next November, and if I do then, I shall be more fortunate than I ever have been in getting news."

The loss of contact between a vessel and its home port brought about a level of anxiety among sailors that was compounded as a ship began its homeward passage. Just as many seamen had despaired of ever seeing America again when they first set sail, so many others on the last leg of their voyages became melancholic and fearful about what had happened while they had been away. Charles Benson, steward on the *Glide,* for instance, found that he could not sleep as he approached his home in Salem, Massachusetts, in 1878. "This uncertainty when I get near home," he wrote, "drives me almost crazy. I am always so, & when I get on shore & most to the house I always find myself trembling all over & some times so faint that I can hardly stand."

For the sailor, then, anxiety was a feature of shipboard life from start to finish. But it was clearly only one discomfort among the many a mariner faced, and the rhetorical question sailors often asked—"who wouldn't sell a farm and go to sea?"—was patently ironic in its intent.

2
Toil and Tribulation: The Rhythms of Shipboard Labor

Can a human being get toughened to all this?

—Robert Weir on the *Clara Bell*, August 22, 1855

One mid-May day in 1859, the whaleship *Atkins Adams* was sailing slowly northward in the Pacific Ocean when the men on her mastheads spotted a vessel behind them. From their height, they could clearly see that the overtaking ship was a clipper. It was midnight when she finally glided past them, and her twenty sails gleamed in the eerie moonlight. Whaleman William Abbe, who described the scene in his diary, noted with awe the clipper's "lofty skysails," "handsome hull," and "handsome decks." For Abbe, though, the sight of the merchant vessel was more painful than pleasing, for it exacerbated the unhappiness he felt with his own ship. "I walked the deck impatient on . . . this laggard barke—& longed to be on a moving quick winged ship," he wrote. Merchant seamen, he claimed, were the only "true sailors," and he ached to be among them.

Abbe's longings were hardly isolated expressions of dissatisfaction. Seamen's journals suggest that the whaleman who did not envy sailors in the merchant service was an exception. And what seemed to generate these feelings of jealousy was the whaleman's recognition, after only a few months at sea, that his work was dirtier, more irregular, and less reliably lucrative than any other deepwater labor. He could not, first of all, count on receiving any money for several years' work. Paid on a curious basis called a "lay" system, he did not earn a monthly wage like a merchant sailor but instead received a share or "lay" of the net profits of the voyage. A foremast hand who was lucky and who remained with his whaleship for three years might sail home to a payment of $150.00. This amounted to monthly earnings of about $4.00—probably half or a third as much as a merchant seaman's wage. And if a whaleman were unlucky, the end of the voyage might find him with no money whatsoever. Most whalemen did not complete a disastrous voyage, however, but left their ships as soon as they sensed financial ruin. Such was the hope, for example, of young Richard Boyenton, a sailor from Salem, Massachusetts, who suffered slow disillusionment on the ship *Bengal*. After cruising five months in the Pacific Ocean in 1834, the *Bengal* had stored a scant thirty gallons of oil, "my share of wich," calculated Boyenton, "is about six and a quater Cents." "I have not as yet concluded," he wrote, "weather to give this as a donation to the sabath school union or to the education foreign mission or Temperance Societies I think However it ought to be the temperance society for we seam as it regards whaleing to have come under the prohibition. . . ." Two months later the whaler was still empty, and Boyenton and his shipmates were disconsolate. The crew, according to the diarist, had "some of the most wo begone countinances here that I ever beheld the dumps and blues predominate by turns but we keep hope ahead. . . ." Like other whalemen who decided that their voyages were wasted efforts, Boyenton eventually gave up his hopes for the *Bengal* and set his sights on returning quickly to port so that he could be discharged. In May 1834, just as he was beginning to dream about new ships and better luck, his captain announced a plan which conflicted with his own:

I have heard to day that our capt intends prolonging this voyage 15 (or 16) months longer if that is the case I hope he will be obliged to drive a Snail through the dismal Swamp in dog dayes with hard peas in his shoes and suck a sponge for nourishment he had ought to have the tooth ache for amusement and a bawling child to rock him to sleepe.

Boats fast to a whale on the Bolus Banks.

Anonymous Sketchbook, n.d.
Kendall Whaling Museum

Boyenton was not the only frustrated whale-man. If there was one recurring complaint in whaling journals, it was that life on cruising grounds was tedious and exasperating in the extreme. The whale chase, which the American public has pictured as the typical scene of the industry, was, in fact, an occasional event which interrupted long weeks of virtual idleness. There was often nothing whatsoever to do on a whaleship. "A whaleman's life," lamented boatsteerer Henry Johnson of the *Acushnet* in 1847,

. . . consists chiefly of eating three times a day & sleeping twelve hours out of the twenty four & loafing about decks the other twelve for month after months.

Some unsuccessful whalemen were so desperate for excitement that they even sought disasters to relieve their ennui. Silliman Ives aboard the *Sunbeam* in 1869 prayed fervently for a storm to provide some adventure: "O that we might see a ship, or ship a sea, either episode being a 'consummation devoutly to be wished.'" Likewise, Captain Samuel Braley on the *Arab* secretly hoped that a man might fall from aloft so that he could enjoy the thrill of an attempted rescue. "I hope that there will be something soon," he confessed in March 1850, "if it is nothing but the cry so shocking to sailors 'man overboard' if we can save him."

Merchant sailors who observed the meanderings of whaleships interpreted their slow progress as a sign of laziness, and frequently spoke of them with disapproval. It was not uncommon for a merchant sailor to remark that a whaleship which ran under shortened sails (a strategy used to remain within a cruising ground) must be commanded by a man who lacked true seamanship. In fact, for merchantmen, whalemen occupied the very bottom of the social hierarchy of deepwater sailors.

A whaleman drives a lance into a dying sperm whale, as another prepares to throw his harpoon. Meanwhile, back on the ship, the smoke and fire indicate that an earlier catch is being tried out. Up in the main masthead a sailor witnesses the various proceedings.

Henry Johnson, *Acushnet*, 1845

Peabody Museum of Salem

This attitude toward whalemen is well-demonstrated by a merchant captain named Charles Emery, who, much to his chagrin, took passage back to America in a whaler in 1839. For Emery, the trip home on the *Columbus* was a voyage of tortured exasperation. Day after day he awoke to the annoying realization that the ship's sails had not been set to take "full advantage" of the wind. On Saturday, May 11, 1839, for instance, he turned out early to discover the "mortifying fact" that the vessel had been running under reefed topsails, where, he was convinced, "royals & top galt studg sails could have been carried with the greatest ease & safty."

Emery was also aggravated by the fact that other vessels had enough canvas out to overtake the whaleship and to pass her with ease. He nearly reached the breaking point one day in June, when a ship which had been sailing near them one night was completely out of sight the next morning:

[We] have not seen o[u]r consort since day before yesterday no wonder if a sailior commands her there are no sailors here, walked the deck in high dudgeon all the morning & have been in no enviable state of mind all day may I never pass another Sunday like it or indeed any other day, Surely the bitter & grevious curse mentioned in the bible must be taking passage home in a whaler may it be an atonement for many sins it is really distressing to me to see the abuse of Gods blessings.

Had Emery been witness to the *Columbus* in real action, when her men were chasing whales or trying them out, his attitude toward whalemen might have been converted to either ad-

Whaling Instruments

Pictured here are the "business ends" of a variety of whaling instruments. From left to right: a lance (used to kill a whale after harpooning it), a two-flued harpoon, a single-flued harpoon, two toggle harpoons, a cutting spade (used to cut blubber from a whale), a porpoise fork, a blubber pick, and a blubber fork.

Twisted Harpoon

This twisted harpoon demonstrates not only the strength of a whale under attack but its tortuous and circuitous efforts to escape. Harpoons were made of malleable rather than brittle metal so that they could be easily straightened and reused.

miration or pity. For, from the moment a whale was spotted from the masthead to the time it was lost or stowed away, a whaleman's work was frenetic and exhausting. Like other men who kept diaries aboard a whaleship, John Martin on the *Lucy Ann* described whale hunts with elaborate detail, explaining how each encounter with the leviathan brought different risks and new, back–breaking tasks. There was the day in the spring of 1842, for example, when Martin's whaleboat succeeded in killing a sperm whale after a long chase only to have it sink. By the time he and his shipmates had pulled the animal to the surface it was late at night, and their ship was nowhere to be seen. Martin's boat then ran into a fog bank so dense, the seaman claimed,

that we could not see the other boats that were only a few fathoms off. We struck a light & hoisted the boats lantern to the end of the boat spreet all hands would then yell together to be heard by the ship. at length we heard a gun which gave us fresh strength, our boat then cut adrift and got aboard & gave directions were the boats were & a breeze springing up we bore away for them & took them aboard after pulling hard from 8 Oclock AM to . . . 10 Oclock PM completely fagged out.

If Martin was "fagged out" after that episode, he was "completely used up" on October 17 after chasing a "devil" of a right whale. This whale "ran" with the whaleboat at the "rate of 60 miles an hour," so fast that water rose up on either side of the boat far above the men's heads: "We could see nothing but a sheet of water all around us. buckets, hats, caps, shoes &c were used to keep the boat free." After this "sleigh ride," the whale sounded and took the boat's line, along with those of two other boats. It was after sundown when Martin and his shipmates finished their work, with nothing to show for it but the loss of 500 fathoms of line and three harpoons.

Only two days later, the *Lucy Ann* was lucky enough to run into another pod of right whales. This time, trouble began when a boatsteerer fastened to a whale. The animal, when he felt the iron, slapped his tail against the boat, knocked it to pieces, and sent the crew flying into the water. The next boat that attempted to lance the whale had even greater problems. As Martin explained:

the waist boat being the next nearest to the whale . . . hauled up to lance him, the whale milled & came head on to the boat. Mr. Dean tried to prick him off by pricking him in the nose with his lance to prevent him from running over the boat . . . when the whale went under water & rose up with the boat on the top of his head it seemed to me as if he raised it up 15 feet out of the water & turned her upside down.

Miraculously, no one was seriously hurt in this episode, even though Henry, one of the oarsmen, was given a ride on a whale's back and Mr. Dean, an officer, suffered seizures on his return to the ship.

While whaleboats were pursuing whales, or being pursued by them, a few men remained on the ship to handle the sails and to keep the vessel within reach of the boats. These individ-

It is not exactly clear why the men of the *Alice* are abandoning their boat, but most likely a whale has threatened them with its flukes, or is beginning a head-on charge. Once they were in the water, the sailors would be picked up by other whaleboats.

Anonymous, *Orray Taft*, c. 1864

Kendall Whaling Museum

As this drawing indicates, blubber is stripped from a whale in much the same way that a fruit is peeled. While the blubber is slowly hoisted, men standing on a cutting stage use sharp, long-handled spades to separate the blubber from the carcass. The men on the left wear harnesses to prevent them from slipping into the shark-infested waters below.

Robert Weir, *Clara Bell,* 1855

Photo: Mystic Seaport Museum

One whaleman, naked at least to his waist, is sunk to his shoulders in the head of a sperm whale as he helps bail oil from the case. This case oil was so pure that it was used commercially in its natural state—and no doubt the sailor who spilled a pail of it, like the one in this scene, was subjected to a stern reprimand.

Robert Weir, *Clara Bell,* 1855

Photo: Mystic Seaport Museum

uals, usually the cook, steward, cooper, or captain, watched the hunt with eager anxiety. The shipmaster of the *Lucy Ann* was even prone to cheerleading, and, according to one sailor, sang the following song to the tune of *Yankee Doodle* when the boats were about to fasten:

O pull my good fellows you dont pull a bit. O you molly horns pull. there he stands up give it to him solid, he's fast, he's fast, he's fast. there he lances him there he spouts thick blood; cocka doodle doo . . .

While killing a whale was cause for celebration, reducing the same animal to oil was not. Ten hours after a whale was brought alongside a ship, most whalemen would confess to their journals that they would be happy if they never saw a spout again. They had good reason, for the nonstop labor involved in peeling the blubber from the whale, cutting it up, trying it out, and, finally, stowing it away was gruesome and hellish.

Several sailor diarists described the event of trying out, but none with the grisly detail of William Abbe aboard the *Atkins Adams.* Thoroughly disgusted with this aspect of whaling by July 17, 1859, he mustered enough fortitude to note his misery in one expressive, almost interminable sentence:

To turn out at midnight & put on clothes soaked in oil—to go on deck & work for Eighteen hours among blubber—slipping—& stumbling on the sloppy decks—till you are covered from crown to heel with oil—Eating with oily hands—oily grub—drinking from oily pots till your mouth & lips have a nauseating oily taste—turning in for a few hours sleep—after wiping off your bare body with oakum to take of the thickest of the oil & then to dream you are under piles of blubber that are heaping & falling upon you till you wake up with a suffocating sense of fear & agony only to hear the eternal clank of the cutting machine &

One sailor transfers oil from a trypot into a cooler, while another moves the cooled oil into a cask for storage. The smell of boiling whale blubber was reputedly nauseating and ships' decks, during the process of cutting in and trying out, were sometimes a foot thick with gurry—a combination of blood, raw blubber, and oil.

Anonymous, *Orray Taft,* c. 1864

Kendall Whaling Museum

the roar of the fires under the try works—or the wind dismally howling through the rigging—to fall asleep only to dream again till you are called on deck to [c]lean off the raw blubber . . . to stand under the lee of the tryworks—cutting up & carrying to casks the soaked & dripping case—till your eyes smart with pain & your mouth is filled with suffocating black smoke from the chimneys—that rools out in thick wretching volumes—to slip in pools of raw oil—to handle hot scraps or boil the boiling oil that splutters and splatters on your face & hands till they burn—to be weary—dirty—oily—sleepy—sick—disgusted with yourself & everybody & everything . . . to go through such a scene—I confess the very thought turns my stomach & dizzies my head—yet I am not foolish enough to wish this vaulable ship to be idle—I hope she will do well—but leave her I must at the next port.

William Abbe did not leave the *Atkins Adams* at the next port—his master refused to discharge him—but even if he had succeeded in jumping ship, he might easily have found the merchant

service a serious disappointment. Merchant sailing may have been more prestigious, more remunerative, and much cleaner than whaling, but its sailors paid dearly for these advantages. First of all, their work was continuously stressful. Their ships, which sometimes carried twice as many sails as whalers, usually had half as many men to handle them. (An average deepwater cargo vessel in the mid-nineteenth century had a crew of fifteen, while a whaleship had twenty-six to thirty.) Their labor was dictated by masters who often had two ambitions: to get their ships to port as fast as possible, and to have them in good repair when they got there. These goals, of course, worked at cross-purposes. For every extra sail that was bent to catch a gust of wind, more canvas ripped, more lines parted, and more repairs had to be made. In rough weather, sailors in a hard-driven merchant vessel were not allowed the alternation of rest and work with "watch and watch" but labored on deck all day, climbing aloft repeatedly to make sail or to shorten it, often in rain, gales, sleet, or snow. In light airs, when they were not repairing the damage from windier days, sailors were ordered to tedious busy work like tarring rigging, slushing spars, scraping rust, painting, or picking oakum. The daily work of a merchant seaman often involved so much drudgery that those men who kept diaries noted it only in

As seaman Henry Tuttle illustrates here, merchant sailors could be just as thrilled to see whales as whalemen were, although for different reasons. Here, the *La-Grange* encounters a pod of large sperm whales, and her sailors point at them in amazement. "Such excitement as there was amongst us," wrote Tuttle, "would make you laugh."

Henry Tuttle, *LaGrange*, 1849
Essex Institute

"All hands reef Topsails".

passing. Horace Putnam, a sailor before the mast on the bark *Cherokee,* recorded his labors on the nineteenth of February, 1848, with a singularly discursive entry:

Up at 7½, ate breakfast till 8 of fried salt pork, with hard biscuit & coffee. Turned too at 8. First, had to lash anchors forward of the windlass (which the day before had been pounded to get the rust off) to keep them from rooling abought The next thing I dong was to splice the throat halyards to the trisail; when finished the helmsman made two bells; the[n] the ship was pumped which has to be done every hour day & night as she leek bad . . . one hundred strokes an hour.

Then, all before 10 A.M., Putnam set the fore and main royal sail and took in the topgallant studding sails. By that time, though, the wind had increased to such an extent that "the fore Royal split in to from head to the foot so there

Slushing (or greasing) spars, along with sweeping decks, making spunyarn, and picking oakum, was one of the most tedious and, consequently, least popular of shipboard jobs.

Edward Haskell, *Tarquin*, 1862

Peabody Museum of Salem

Isaac Baker illustrates the delights of repairing a rope with both hands while clinging to the royal mast, high above the ship's deck, with both feet.

Isaac Baker, *Tuskar*, 1842

Private Collection

was another job. I went aloft and sent down the yard, which took the rest of the forenoon to repair At twelve, or noon got our dinner then went below."

The *Cherokee*'s aggressive performance under sail taxed her sailors, but they were accustomed to such work. Whalemen, like those on the *William Gifford*, on the other hand, were used to conservative sail changes, and when they were supplied with a merchant master as their captain they were astonished by his demands. The speed with which he drove the vessel left them gasping with exhaustion from making and taking in sail all day long. "We have had bad weather ever since we left Tahiti," complained a tired hand named Edward Kirwin in June 1872, "and carried sail in regular merchantman style (lee rail under) and not take it in till the last minute. About all our rigging is rotten and keeps us moving all the time repairing it."

Popular histories have suggested that for heavy labor aboard ships like the *William Gifford* and the *Cherokee*, sailors sang an appropriate shanty that eased their task. The truth, at least from the testimony of these journals, seems to be that only some merchantmen had shantymen to direct rhythmic work songs; on other merchant ships, and on whalers, the burden of shipboard work was shouldered without benefit of music.

Perhaps even more difficult for merchant sailors to endure than the continuous toil of changing sails were the all-too-frequent becalmings. If sailors were unhappy with the extra labor attendant on windy weather, they at least appreciated the fact that they were moving forward, but in a calm, the miseries and tedium of performing menial tasks were compounded. Thus, even though merchant seamen were paid on a daily basis, and every day for them meant more money, they always hoped to shorten passages as much as possible and to get into port. For the shipmaster, long passages not only meant an embarrassing loss of money for the owners but a threat to his reputation for aggressive seamanship.

Becalmed sailors were prolific in expressing their frustrations. Isaac Baker on the ship *Merrimac* from Boston to Melbourne found special

Ship *George* from *Salem* towards *Calcutta*

H.	K.	H.K.	Courses.	Winds.	Lee.	Remarks. Tuesday Oct. 18th

Begins hard Gales with a large sea at 2. P.M. Call'd all hands, furl'd Mainsail, Jib, & Mizen Topsail.
at 3. Set Staysails, and got preventer braces on F. and Main Yards.
" 6. Close reef't the Fore Topsail, hauld down Staysails, and scud her, under the Foresail & close reef'd F. & Main Topsails, till 8. A.M. two hands at the Helm. from 8 to 12. all say that they never see sail carried so before.
at 6. A.M. very heavy squalls, with Hail
" 9. Set the close reef's from F. & M. Topsails set reef'd Mainsail, Jib & close reef'd Mizen Topsail. Latter Part, more moderate, let down reef's from the Topsails, and set M.T. & Jib Sail
Long. by Chro[n]. 58 52. East.—

Course.	Dist.	Diff. lat.	Dep.	Lat. by D. R.	Lat. by Ob.	Varia.	Diff. Long.	Long. in.	Long. by Ob.
N 81 E	224	34 N	219 E	38 53	38 55	27 E	4 42	53 40	East

H.	K.	H.K.	Courses.	Winds.	Lee.	Remarks. Wednesday Oct. 19th

First Part, fresh Breezes, and

eloquence in recounting his bout with baffling winds. On May 6, 1858, Baker was beginning to sound exasperated as he noted in his journal that the early, middle, and latter parts of his day had all been characterized by calm weather. By May 9, when the weather persisted, he was beside himself:

The Calm yet remains—the water is calm, the sky is calm, the Petrel fly calmly along, a few Bonitos swim calmly around and calmly refuse to bite. Calm humanity discouraged by the calmness of nature gets obstreperous and vents its spleen in anything but a

Clearly, the master of the merchant ship *George* liked to carry as much sail as he could. A log entry from October 18, 1831 shows how hard his seamen worked to change sails in a heavy gale.

Andrew Haraden, *George,* 1831

Peabody Museum of Salem

calm & contented manner—the very sails of the ship flap calmly against the masts while [the] yards & spars agonizingly creak & shriek (calmly as possible) at irregular intervals and with no regard to the feelings of any unwilling listener—harsh notes which can only be interrupted and unmusically written thus C-A-L-M.

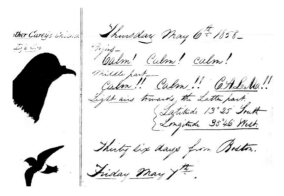

Isaac Baker, *Merrimac*, 1858
Private Collection

For many merchant seamen, hard work did not stop when they entered port, and taking in and discharging cargo was often just as difficult as transporting it. Here, sailors in Brazil struggle to load bulls into their vessel. According to the diarist, once these animals were aboard, the seamen had to pour vinegar in their nostrils to prevent them from sitting down and hurting themselves.

William C. Taylor, *Angelia*, 1862
Essex Institute

Calms always yielded to brisk winds eventually, and vessels made their way into port. But while merchant sailors of every rank enjoyed some liberty and sighed with relief at the change of scene, their work and their waiting were not entirely at an end. Seamen who remained with their ships usually went to work on repairs or helped discharge or load cargo. Shipmasters exchanged the anxieties of a calm for those of waiting for orders to see where they would sail next. Even though they had driven their vessels as fast as possible to make port, they were forced to mark time once they were there. Sooner or later, of course, their vessels were loaded, their orders were delivered, a new crew was shipped, and they weighed anchor. Then the days of toil and tribulation and the demanding rhythms of seafaring labor began once again.

'DEPARTURE,

William Haskell, *Marcella*, c. 1836

Nicholson Whaling Collection

Merchant sailors, like the one pictured here leaning on
the capstan, usually worked two hour shifts on lookout
when they kept a sharp eye out for passing ships, sub-
merged obstacles, changing weather, and land. Whalemen, who wanted to see as much of the ocean as possible in their search for prey, stood their lookouts on
perches (called mast-heads) up to one hundred feet
above the ship's deck.

Edward Haskell, *Tarquin*, 1862

Peabody Museum of Salem

Anonymous, *Orray Taft*, c. 1864

Kendall Whaling Museum

Anonymous, *Orray Taft*, c. 1864
Kendall Whaling Museum

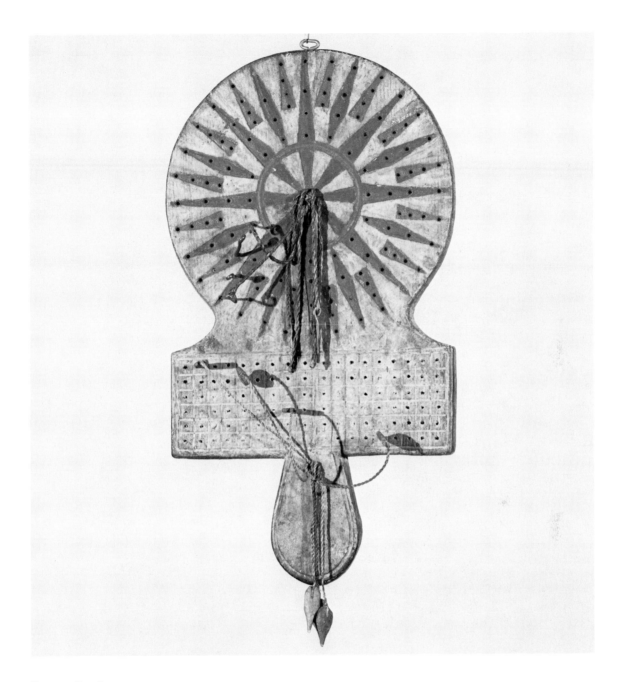

Traverse Board

While foremast hands were changing sails, steering, or performing busy work, chief officers, when not ordering seamen, were attending to the ship's navigation. During the nineteenth century, a vessel's position was determined either by making astronomical observations with instruments or, if skies were overcast, by dead reckoning. With dead reckoning, sailors judged position by taking account of speed attained, courses set, and distances run. During a watch, a sailor could keep track of the courses he steered by making notations on a slate, or by relying on a traverse board like the one above. He used the board by inserting a peg into a hole by a compass point every half hour. At the end of a watch the average course sailed could be determined by the position of pegs. The traverse board pictured here is a rare example from nineteenth century America.

Sailmaker's Bag

Sailmakers had a range of specialized equipment at
their disposal, including some of the tools contained in
this canvas bag: fids for splicing rope (top), wooden
thimble, seam rubber (right center), sailmaker's palm
(center), horn cup with grease, needlecases, and an
awl.

3
Hot Tempers and Ill Winds

Now men! You are bound on a long voyage, and you must have no quarreling, no striking each other. If there is any striking to be done, I am the one to do it.

—Stephen Curtis (quoting Captain Dennis Haskell) on the ship *Mercury,* May 25, 1841

At the beginning of a voyage, nearly every shipmaster issued a command like Captain Haskell's, exhorting seamen to work in cooperation and to live in peace. But no matter how amicable a ship's company might be when a vessel left port, it was only a matter of time before the combined elements of tedium and temper made the forward and aftercabins seethe with hostility.

Even though the allegiances of mariners changed constantly, the ship's steward and cook were frequent targets of shipboard enmity. Men of these ranks stimulated the belligerence of many sailors not only because they could rarely satisfy the ship's culinary needs, but because of their race. Crew lists indicate that most stewards and cooks on deepwater vessels in the mid-nineteenth century were black. Racial slurs abound in these white sailors' diaries, and journals indicate that disciplinary action against black seamen was more frequent and more severe than that against whites. Ships' officers, often on appeal from the crew, doled out severe corporal punishments to cooks and stewards for such offenses as "wasting" or "hoarding" food, for burning duff or boiling rotten eggs, or for "dirtiness." On one occasion, the cook of the ship *Columbus* in 1852 was force-fed a pudding he had prepared for the entire crew because he had scorched it.

As eager as many sailors were to start trouble

with cooks and stewards, they were just as willing to fight among themselves, as numerous reports of bloody noses, fist fights, and stabbings in the forecastle attest. The division of a ship's crew into watches provided a natural framework for competition between sailors. This competition manifested itself in contests as benign as boat races, but it occasionally turned into outright warfare. Such was the case on the ship *Atkins Adams* when the two watches began a rivalry in January 1859 to determine which could best disturb the other's sleep by jumping up and down on deck. One sailor, nicknamed "the Growler," was chosen as a major target for abuse, but he decided to stop the whole proceedings with a fist fight, which then turned into a serious battle with belaying pins.

Much to the delight and amusement of forecastle sailors, shipmasters and mates were regularly at odds with one another. While officers may have tried to hide this high-level friction, their disagreements were occasionally public, and several seamen noted the pleasure of hearing an argument between their superiors. On the ship *Arab* William Stetson described the growl his skipper and mate had on June 9, 1855 as being "highly relished" by his shipmates. And on the whaleship *Mercury* in 1842 seamen surreptitiously stationed themselves near their captain and mate in order to hear a quarrel. "During the hottest of the fun," explained diarist Stephen Curtis, "a keen observer might have noticed some dozen or fifteen men crouched forward of the tryworks, enjoying a fit of laughter (so as not to be heard) at what they called 'fun.' Nothing suited better than to have the two first officers of the ship at variance with each other."

Although friction could exist on a ship between and among any faction, it became most virulent and violent when it occurred between those who officially had the most power and those who had the least—the officers and the crew. When a sailor signed shipping articles and promised to be a "good and faithful" seaman, he relinquished his rights to individual freedom. Not only did he have to obey the rules and commands of his officers without question, he could not enter any complaint without being considered mutinous. And for mutiny he could be pun-

Shorty says the meat smells —
Skinner swears the Pork is good

By far the most frequent altercations on shipboard concerned the distribution, the quantity, and the quality of food. In a case like the one illustrated here, an officer would intervene and, almost inevitably, would punish the cook.

Captain James Skinner?, *Concordia,* 1867

Nicholson Whaling Collection

---

ished and imprisoned and, up to 1835, put to death. Furthermore, any attempt on his part to break the contract of shipping articles and to desert ship was an imprisonable offense. A sailor, therefore, once he signed articles, was bound to the voyage in many ways.

In addition to obeying federal regulations, seamen were expected to comply with any idiosyncratic rules a shipmaster wanted to enforce. Shortly after sailing, a captain often called his hands together for a short "talk," in which he encouraged them to obey his orders and to "behave." On some ships the master supplemented this lecture with a written list of his own rules. On the bark *William Schroder,* for instance, the afterguard sent forward the following prescription for proper sailor behavior:

"Rules for the Bark Wm Schroder"

"No Swearing alowed on board" "No Sleeping in the watch on deck" "No long Yarns while at work" "No Work on the Sabbath" "No Towing of clothes" "Be active in taking in and making sail "Spend as little time as possible in getting on deck when the watch or all hands are calld and by so doing you will receive good language and good usuage . . .

What sailors could expect in the way of restrictions and regulations obviously differed from ship to ship. While all American sea captains in the mid-nineteenth century were officially enjoined by shipping articles to prohibit "ardent spirits" on board, many carried liquor for the aftercabin's pleasure and for the occasional bracing of sailors during rough weather, hard work, or holidays. Some masters, though, were prohibitionists, and they not only kept their ships free of alcohol, but encouraged their crews to sign the temperance pledge. Others refused to allow seamen to dance, to play cards, or to throw dice, and limited them to quieter, less competitive forms of amusement. Sailors with such captains were, of course, the objects of pity to mariners who spent their free time in card games and who gambled and danced to their hearts' content.

Even though some masters relaxed various social or moral rules on shipboard, no sea captain was flexible when it came to laws governing respect for his authority. For every nose that an officer bloodied for a sailor's physical misbehavior, he struck two for insolent language or "talking back." Battles of will between officers and seamen over verbal insubordination were almost everyday events, and the conflicts that occurred when an officer was unable to elicit a proper expression of humility were painful and prolonged. Captain Avery F. Parker resorted to flogging a sailor on the *Midas* in 1843 because the man repeatedly refused to answer him in a deferential manner. As Parker explained in his journal:

[I] asked him again if he would answer me civilly for the future, he replied he would answer me as he allways had, I told him he did not answer my question . . . I gave him in all, four half Doz. of lashes at intervals of ten or twelve minutes, asking him between each two half dozen, if he would Answer me civilly.

Anonymous, *Orray Taft*, c. 1864
Kendall Whaling Museum

Eventually the sailor's resistance was broken, and he terminated his punishment by a simple "Yes sir."

In 1850, seven years after Parker whipped his sailor into submission, flogging on American vessels "of commerce" was prohibited by federal statute. While this did not prevent some masters from using the rope's end to discipline sailors, many sea captains turned to irons instead and used leg and wrist irons together for the most serious offenders.

To supplement the rope and the irons, ship-masters invented a wide variety of punishments.

The captain of the *Canada* kept his steward sealed in a barrel for two weeks in 1846 after the seaman cut some of the ship's stays. According to diarist Sylvanus Tallman, the prisoner was taken out only for an occasional "airing" before he was dropped ashore. On the ship *Columbus* in 1837, Captain Benjamin Ellis seized two men who had been fighting and devised a punishment to fit their crime: he tied their left hands together, gave them pieces of rope, and had them whip each other "untill they were tired." The master then rounded out the punishment himself by giving the men three blows apiece.

Some of the shipmasters who eschewed corporal punishment disciplined seamen by assign-

Leg and Wrist Irons

Brass Knuckles and Sling Shot

While the sling shot could have served a number of purposes, the brass knuckles had only one lethal function—to give a human blow as much power as possible.

Colt Revolver

A revolver like this one, manufactured at the Colt factory in Hartford between 1851 and 1865, could have been purchased by any shipmaster for about $24.00 in 1855. It is a .36 caliber gun, and has a naval battle engraved on its cylinder. The revolving cylinder was one of Colt's inventions, and he is said to have drawn the inspiration for it during a sailing voyage from Boston to Calcutta in 1830, when he observed the clutch system of a ship's wheel.

ing them menial "boys'" tasks like scraping iron work, washing decks, or, on whalers, scrubbing trypots. Others dealt with sailors' disobedience by restricting their most basic rights: sleep, food, wages, or liberty.

It was difficult for a sailor to predict exactly what action a shipmaster might take in response to specific infractions. While most major crimes, such as mutiny or desertion, had prescribed fines or lengths of imprisonment that were enforced in port, almost all other offenses were settled by shipmasters at sea, where their judgments were often influenced by external factors. When a sea captain was aggravated by headwinds or poor whaling, his even-handedness was sometimes seriously impaired. The men of the bark *Brothers,* for example, suffered undue reprimands on March 20, 1866, because it was Captain Weekes's birthday and he wished he were at home with his family. The shipmaster noted in his diary that he found a solution to his melancholia by going on deck, where he "picked all the flaws [he] could, work done over &c, felt better." In a similar manner, mate Ambrose Bates on the *Nimrod* punished a sailor because he was frustrated and bored with sea life. "Sometimes [I] feel cross," he wrote in 1861, "then of cours evrybody does not suit well then what. why stand clear Thunder and lightning. I thrashed a man this morning and now I rearly feel sorrowly for doing so . . ."

Occasionally a shipmaster allowed his personal weaknesses to completely overwhelm his professional obligations and duties. If his failings were recognized and buffered by his junior officers, then the success of the voyage was not threatened. Such was the case with Bates's captain, William Heath. In October 1860, Heath, who was suffering from delirium and alcohol withdrawal, had to be humored and managed by his mates to prevent him from endangering either himself or his crew. "Capt Heath is visited with the blue devils," noted Bates in his journal.

His rum has been gone some four or five days unless he has had some privetly which I doubt He has seen this afternoon a sort [of] devils made up of old cloths . . . It is hoped that he will soon be better for the ship must soon pass a chain of dangerous islands and something must be done for the safty of our lives and ship He also thretens to shoot somebody Not a very pleasant thing to be used by a crazy-man in a ships Cabin among so many people.

On the following day, although Heath hallucinated that a Russian coat was a human being and that there were women on the ship, his officers sensed that he was recovering. By October twelfth the captain was a different man. Bates explained that "everything seems to be new to him He is very much interested in his business, and has taken to reading the papers which have been in the ship all the season. . . ."

Even if William Heath had continued to behave like a madman, his officers would probably have been reluctant to remove him forcibly from the ship's command. Seafarers' journals indicate that sailors, both lesser officers and crew, tolerated long periods of abuse before making any major attempts to resist the authority of a shipmaster. In the one case of mutiny among the voyages described here, the shipmaster all but destroyed the ship, the voyage, his officers, and his crew before the foremast hands staged a successful revolt. This troubled ship was the *William Gifford,* and her problems stemmed from her captain's constant need for women. In one year, between 1871 and 1872, according to foremast hand Edward Kirwin, Captain Richard Veeder interrupted his whaling cruise in the Pacific to visit women ashore for 49 days and to bring prostitutes aboard for a total of 210 days. There was no time to hunt for whales, and the captain was hardly eager to look for them. His daily activities revolved around his female guests. He played cards with them; he washed their clothes; he made squirt guns for them to play with. Kirwin grumbled about his captain's behavior, but it was only when Veeder's obsessions took a particularly malevolent turn that he and other crew members finally acted. On May 19, 1872, the captain's favorite woman ran into the forecastle, claiming that the captain "had been beating her" and that he was loading his revolvers to kill her. The crew rushed to capture Veeder, bound him, and told their officers to steer for the nearest consul at Tahiti. There, their case was quickly heard, Veeder and the women were removed from the ship, and a new master was placed in charge of the vessel.

The *William Gifford* story, among other accounts of shipboard conflict, makes it clear that sailors were reluctant to make violent changes in the formal order of a ship's command. Seamen's diaries indicate, though, that sailors had more power on a vessel than is generally imagined. Even though collective bargaining and striking were imprisonable offenses in the 1800s, seamen did manage to assert some control on shipboard by collective action. They frequently succeeded in avoiding work, for example, by feigning illness, or, as sailors called it, by "sogering" or "playing possum." Because so many seamen were legitimately sick, a shipmaster often had difficulty determining the truth of a mariner's complaint and let some malingerers rest. Sometimes, however, sailors' attempts to avoid work backfired, as they did on the *Columbus* in 1851 when the captain forced radical treatment on his "sick" sailors. He gave one man, according to journal–keeper Edwin Pulver, a "heavy dose of saults," and another a "blister of spanish flies mixed with pepper sauce." Rather than endure another round of medicine, these men went immediately to their duty. Pulver, the third mate, was convinced of the necessity of his master's aggressive action:

On boad of a whaleship where we have No doctor the crew will try to take the advantage and play the sick man with out a cause but there looks most allways betrays them and then the ownly way is to give them the most disagreeable drugs which will make them sick anyhow wether they wish to be or Not we are sure to have them to there duty in Short meter. The 2 men that the Captain has cured in 6 hours would off laid below for weeks if they had been Nursed and humored as a sick man would be.

Unlike Pulver's captain, other shipmasters recognized the dangers of ignoring a possibly sick man. Captain Samuel Braley, for one, knew that the repercussions of neglecting a sick crewman might extend all the way back home and for this reason indulged one of his sailors who claimed to be ill. As he explained:

although he mite be well and I have evry reason to believe that he was so at the time he mite be taken realy sick in one hour afterward and then what a cry there would be raised against the Capt of the three masted ship . . . there are always enough on shore to listen to jacks yarns, and put more reliance in it than

they would in everything that the master and all his officers could say.

The fears of shipmasters like Braley meant that occasionally sailors could and did avoid their duty. But while feigning illness might work with the captain, it did not always succeed with the rest of the crew. Any man who did not accept his share of the work placed additional burdens on other sailors, and they made sure that he deserved his rest or paid some penalty. A member of the crew of the *Lucy Ann* who decided in 1842 that he was unable to take his turn at cleaning the forecastle received a slight but decisive "tap" from one of the older members of the crew as an encouragement to participate in the work in the future. And on several other vessels, crew members who slept through their watches were made the butts of painful practical jokes. A typical scene occurred on the bark *Baltic* in February 1857. According to J. E. Haviland:

We had considerable sport in our morning watch, we turned out at 3 AM as usual (when our 8 hours on Deck) all except one of our watch, who says he did not hear the Watch called. It is the fashion when any of us do not hear the watch called to let them lay & in a short time one of us comes down in the Forecastle with a long rope leaving one end on Deck and with the other End they made fast to the fellows leg or foot that is innocently sleeping in his Bunk then all hands on Deck haul with all their might, endangering life, and limb.

Occasionally foremast hands decided to work collectively to achieve some goal, and they had their greatest successes when their shipmasters were most vulnerable. In a port where a captain would have difficulty procuring another crew, sailors demanded liberty and freedom ashore

According to one journal keeper, one of the "most Terrifick encounters between man and man" occurred when a sailor named Loony Pete walked up to "plug ugly" Sam Crow and spat in his eye. Crow dared him to do it three more times, which he did, and the fight was on. The match was fairly even until the third round, when Pete hit Crow "somewhere between the right eye and the left big toe" and sent him down "with the words Martha Jane slowly oozing from his mouth."

Anonymous, *Orray Taft*, 1865
Kendall Whaling Museum

Round 1st

Round 2 nd

Round 3 d

Round 4th

last Round

Tremenduos Battle between
Sam, Crow and Loony Pet

with little fear that they would be locked in jail for long. The power of a crew aboard an endangered ship was also immense. This is best demonstrated by the case of the ship *Rambler* when, in November 1855 in the middle of the South Pacific Ocean, the vessel sprung a leak. The master, Captain Winchester, wanted to sail the ship to Talcahuano, Chile, for repairs and from there to ship his oil home. The crew decided otherwise. On November twenty-sixth they marched aft to the captain and refused to pump the ship—then leaking 100 strokes every five minutes—and declared their intention of sailing into the nearest port. ". . . After some more words on the subject," wrote seaman James Payne, "we came forward to give him a chance to make up his mind to let the ship sink or go into port at 8½ oclock he gave orders to square the yards and keep the ship S b[y] W." The seamen had won the dispute, and on December seventh the ship safely reached Upola, in the Navigator Islands, where it was condemned after a survey.

By far the most effective leverage sailors had over their captain was the ability to damage his reputation. Many shipmasters were almost paranoid about their "characters" and strongly respected a sailor's ability to gossip in port. They knew that seamen could not only damage their recruitment efforts by spreading word of their dissatisfactions to potential crew members, but that they could also formally protest against them to the consul. The possibility of later reprisal by the master was unimportant to the sailor who deserted or gained a discharge.

It is clear from captains' diaries that the need to guard their reputations among seamen governed some of their behavior on shipboard. When the crew of the bark *Reaper* became drunk and unruly in port in March 1838, Captain Benjamin Neal was paralyzed as a disciplinarian because: ". . . if I had struck them or used any harsh means it wold have bin a fine hande for them in Salem." And on the *Persia* in 1848 mate Beriah Manchester was disgusted by the importance his captain attached to his reputation in his handling of the crew: "His only wish is to get the name of a Cleaver man by the Chrew he will allow Boath cardes and Dice paid

on deck in the day time and fiteing in boath day and night."

Shipmasters were also sensitive to what people at home might say if they mistreated a man. The second mate on the *Eliza Mason* escaped punishment for a variety of offenses because he was from Martha's Vineyard, the captain's home port, and Captain Jernegan feared gossip. Orson Shattuck, the journal keeper, commented in 1854 that "she [Mrs. Jernegan] and the Capt endure it all because they [are] afraid his ma would feel bad or that some of the old grannies, and young misses in pantaletts in Edgartown would say that Capt J was too strict and too severe and did not treat him well."

From time to time, hometown connections worked against a sailor, especially when a shipmaster suspected he was the subject of unflattering reports. On the bark *Ceres* on April 19, 1835, sailors who had written letters home from Oahu were prevented from sending them by the captain. As seaman John Cleland explained in his journal: "We did not get our letters sent as we expected the old man not choosing to let them go ashore for fear we had been writing about him."

The captain of a merchant vessel bound to Sydney from Boston seemed to have been equally worried about the wagging tongues of his sailors. "I think the Captain is affraid we are talking about him," wrote seaman Henry Davis, "for he walks the main deck from morning till night and watches us as sharp as a cat watches a mouse." Davis was another sailor who found that knowing his shipmaster was not entirely helpful. Both men were from Cape Cod, and, according to Davis, the captain expected the sailor to inform him of any discontentment in the forecastle and to warn him of any impending desertions "as if I shipped for a spy." Not only did Davis not receive any special treatment through his connections, but his request for a discharge was flatly denied. The captain claimed that he had promised the sailor's mother he

Anonymous, *Orray Taft*, c. 1864
Kendall Whaling Museum

t to a between the Steward and cook.

would bring him back in the ship. Frustrated by his master's solicitousness, Davis asserted in his journal that he "wished the ship had sunk before I had come in her." "If I ever go another long voyage," he vowed, "and I don't much think I shall if this is a fair specimen of them—I will go with a man I never heard of before, so that I can do what I would like to without being afraid of having it brought up when we get Home. . . ."

No doubt many masters shared Davis's sentiments and were grateful for whatever anonymity they could find. Even when shipmasters sailed with a crew of new and strange faces, however, there were other ghosts of home that they carried with them. An almost universal desire of commanding officers was to be seen as successful by the public. The fear that their professional efforts might be an advertised failure haunted many whaling masters, who might, with the worst possible luck, return with no oil at all. "It is not only the dollars and cents, But a mans character depends on his good or Bad fortune in the eyes of the Public," explained Captain George Gardner in 1843, when he had very few whales to his name. Captain Joseph Dias felt similar anguish when, after he had been out of New Bedford on the *Pocohantas* for over a year, he had only tried out 150 barrels of oil. "What will people think at home to hear from me 13 mos out with nothing," he asked in 1851, "I don't know as I have done any thing to be ashamed of for God knows I have done my best to get a voyage."

The captain of the *Ceres* was so embarrassed by his bad luck that he went to extraordinary lengths to maintain the appearance of a successful voyage, when in fact his vessel was two-thirds empty. On September 18, 1837, as the *Ceres* was nearing her home port of Wilmington, Delaware, the captain took in over one hundred barrels of sea water to lower the vessel in the water to simulate a full ship. "This looks rather blank," commented seaman John Cleland, "decieving the people of Wilmington with the flattering hopes of our returning home in 30 months, with a full cargo. . . ."

Whalemen were quite aware of the crucial importance of a full ship to their masters, and they used this knowledge to significant advantage. One of the most effective means of gaining power on a whaleship was to refuse to pull for, or to harpoon a whale. Since masters could not easily differentiate between hard luck and intentional clumsiness, it was difficult for them to punish men for not capturing whales. It was easy for sailors, on the other hand, to punish their shipmasters by withholding their efforts on whaling grounds. Even though they, too, might suffer financial loss by allowing whales to go free, the money they took home at the end of the voyage was often so negligible that it did not serve as much of a deterrent to their obstructive behavior.

While the dispensation of rewards and punishments on shipboard clearly fell to the afterguard, then, the pattern of power on a deepwater sailing vessel was a complicated one. Shipmasters usually had the final say in disputes and had the authority of consuls and shipping articles behind them. But sailors took control of the vessel more than is commonly believed, not through violent mutiny but through carefully timed resistance to authority.

4
The Pleasures and Rites of Passage

My opinion is that any man who has a log hut on land with a corn cake at the fire and would concent to leave them to come to the Sooloo Sea . . . is a proper subject for a lunatic Asylum.

—Marshall Keith on the bark *Brewster*, 1864

With all the aggravations of shipboard life and labor, it is a wonder that any man in his right mind would have signed shipping articles and elected to sail. The seemingly obvious answer is that, as Marshall Keith suggests, very few clear-headed men *would* have chosen such an existence and that most men who found themselves on deep water were there by force, having been shanghaied. Indeed, the shipping of drunk or destitute men against their wills is a simple explanation for vessels with full crews. The testimony of these diaries, however, suggests that for the men who sailed from the East Coast in the mid-1800s, being shanghaied was not a common threat. In fact all of these diary keepers—even the most destitute—claimed that the decision to go to sea, as regrettable as it may sometimes have been, was theirs alone. A sailor named Abram Briggs spoke for scores of others when he grimly accepted the responsibility for his voyage. "I have put my foot In It & I have got to put up with It," he wrote on the *Eliza Adams* in 1873. "Grin & bear It. grin & bear It Is the only remedy." If these sailors, then, did sign shipping articles of their own accord, what prompted them to do so?

Strange as it may seem, a small number of first-time mariners were actually attracted to seafaring because it promised them hardship and deprivation. These men usually had the means or training for other professions, but, for a variety of reasons, wanted some years of self-exile. A few of them, like Harvard law student William Abbe, went for their health, hoping that fresh winds and hard labor would make them physically stronger. Others sought to improve their souls instead of their bodies and banished themselves from society as an exercise in reform and self-punishment. One such was Elias Trotter from Albany, New York, who left for a voyage on the ship *Illinois* in 1845 because he had committed, in his mind at least, a sin "in a manner unparalled." Every day of arduous work at sea brought Trotter not frustration or anger, but exhilaration through pain. "I would not have changed my situation as a sailor before the mast on the good ship Illinois," he noted in his journal in October 1845, "encountering dangers everyday, liable to toil & hardship, for home its gaiety, its pleasure, its comfort. And the reason is, that here everyday, I am confident of learning something & moreover a great thing, that of self-denial. . . ."

Orson Shattuck, a New Hampshire man, looked for the same kind of absolution through seafaring. He, too, had committed some unpardonable (and inexpressible) sin, and he hoped that life aboard the *Eliza Mason* would make him a "better man." He would, as he explained in his diary in October 1850, "dole out a life of repentance and misery among strangers."

For Shattuck and Trotter, the life of a sailor was penance for past sins. For other men it was a deterrent to future misconduct. Trotter's best friend aboard the *Illinois* was a former overseer in a large Maine mill who found that going to sea was the only way to avoid liaisons with female mill workers. Likewise, Charles Benson, a steward on the merchant bark *Glide* in 1878, maintained that he could not stay at home long because there were "too many temptations."

Another man who claimed to be in "need" of abstinence was one Dan Whitfield, who signed aboard the *Doctor Franklin* in 1856. Whitfield declared in his journal that sailing was the only cure for his alcoholism. "I began to tremble for my life, Both here and here after," he explained before sailing.

For this reason, I came to New Bedford; Three things alone, I well knew was that could keep me from the

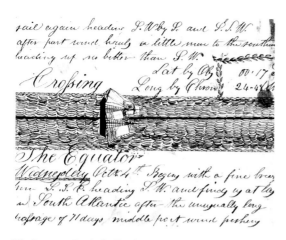

Washington Fosdick, *Emeline*, 1843
Photo: Old Dartmouth Historical Society

Curse that lies heavily upon me! State Prison, A Man of War, or a Whaler. I chose the latter . . . I cared not if I made any money on the Voyage or not; If I can only cure myself of my evil habit, by going this voyage, I shall think myself more than amply repaid for the time spent in accomplishing it. And May God! in his infinite Mercy Enable me to Perform this voyage.

There were a few men, then, who looked forward to the discomforts of seafaring. Most, however, went to sea despite hardships, not because of them. Many, lured either by propaganda or past experience, had grand plans for the cash rewards of their trips. They planned to support wives, to marry for the first time, or to buy houses or farms. Needless to say, most of these optimists were destined for sad disappointments. Why, then, if financial reward was their object but voyages rarely made them rich, would some men sign on ships again? The explanation offered by returning seamen was that sailing actually meant more than money. It offered emotional sustenance—it guaranteed distant locations that were romantic and sublime, opportunities for excitement and danger, and a life of constant change. For a few of these men, seafaring was the only remedy for a roving disposition.

Perhaps the most incurable case of restless temperament was that of thirty-five-year-old Ambrose Bates, who sailed again and again as a mate on long whaling voyages to the Pacific. Bates, from coastal New England, had a wife and young son at home whom he loved deeply. He could not, however, be home with them for long before he became unhappy and restless. As he explained in a journal to his wife in 1867:

Over and over again and I do not know but it always will be my lot to live in uneasiness In vain I have sough[t] a place upon the globe that I might settle down in quiet contentment But alas none has yet lured me from the wild inclination for roaming And although I have been blessed with all the heart could ask still as it seems almost against my will I find myself vointeerly flying from all I love on earth.

Bates could only think of one solution to his predicament—to persuade Annie, his wife, and Orrie, his son, to move with him from city to city while he "drove some business that would pay." This, he thought, might satisfy his "roveing nature."

What enamored Bates of ship life, besides its motion, was its potential for danger. He was not the only man, of course, who thrilled to the sound of crashing waves and foaming billows. Many sailors felt exhilarated by even the most violent of ocean storms, and yearned, when on land, to be in a more precarious place. Silliman Ives, for example, found the sight of a wind-swept ocean the most powerful call to sea he knew. "How many times," Ives noted in 1868,

after a long stop on shore have I found my way to some spot where I could look out upon old ocean, and with the roar of the breakers in my ears and the ships as they went dancing over the waves visible to my eyes, there has come over me such a longing, such a desire to once more feel a deck under my feet, and to be tossed and tumbled about by old Neptune once again, as would scarcely by satisfied by all the inducements which a sojourn on terra firma could offer.

Sailors not only appreciated gales and hurricanes but more peaceful weather as well. Sunrises and sunsets at sea provoked much admi-

---

Isaac Baker, as mate of the *Tarquin,* was able to record the Neptune visit that Edward Haskell underwent as an initiate.

Isaac Baker, *Tarquin,* 1862
Private Collection

Y^e Monarch of Y^e Ocean.

Resignation.

Treachery.

Congratulation

Initiation Implements

From left to right: oversized wooden razor, wooden bucket with panbone handle from the bark *Lancer,* brass speaking trumpet, porpoise fork.

ration among mariners. Horace Putnam, a foremast hand on the *William Schroder* in the 1840s, found sunsets on deep water to be "truly beautiful. sublime." And Charles Austin, on the ship *Charles Phelps,* discovered a sky so "serene" on the twenty-sixth of October, 1842, that he thought that "no pa[i]nter could paint it more beautiful as far as the eye can extend there is not a cloud to be seen." Here, he added, "is the pleasure of sailors."

To some men, then, sailing granted satisfaction with its pain. It delivered excitement, sublimity, and the chance to dream about, if not realize, financial success. And there were other benefits, too. Seafaring gave men a chance to participate in a society that was, for all its difficulties, quite select. The young man who sailed into the southern hemisphere brought home strange souvenirs and exotic stories that no youth traveling to New York City could rival, and sailors were well aware that their foreign travels impressed provincial friends and relatives.

Besides achieving a kind of elitism through worldliness, sailors also acquired an exclusive language and technology. "Learning the ropes" marked them as members of a special class of professionals. But even though the transformation of a landsman into a sailor might begin as soon as a man reefed topsails for the first time, it was not complete until he crossed the equator. There, in an event sometimes celebrated formally and sometimes not, all greenhands achieved a status that no landsman could share: they became Sons of Neptune.

For those ships' crews who celebrated the Neptune ritual, the weather was usually just right. The temperature was hot and humid and the winds light and variable. Sailors, anxious to get to cruising grounds or to port, were eager for diversion. Even before a ship reached 0° latitude, experienced seamen began to tease greenhands about their upcoming trial and to work on their credulity. They tried, first of all, to convince new sailors that the equator was a visible line, and they sometimes succeeded. On the *Clara Bell,* for instance, Robert Weir reported that the other greenhands not only expected to see the line but to find it serving several useful purposes. "We are near the line as Everyone calls the Equator," he wrote in 1855. "The Green ones on board expect to see it, and probably find hanging thereon clothes as in ones back yard, or boobys and other birds roosting upon it. . . ."

Some time before the ceremony, Neptune usually appeared in costume to announce his forthcoming visit. This had the effect of working the new sailors up to a high pitch of excitement, which was relieved only by anxiety as the time for their trial drew near. A number of diarists provided accounts of the ritual but none with the enthusiasm of Edward Haskell, a young boy from Newburyport, Massachusetts, who was bound on a pepper voyage to the East Indies. On a rainy but calm April 29, 1862, three weeks after leaving Boston, Haskell's ship, the *Tarquin,* crossed the equator. Some time in the middle of the afternoon, a sailor went aloft to look for approaching ships. Curiously enough, he immediately sighted a sail very close by. Haskell tells us the rest:

He had scarcely been up a minute before he sang out "Sail ho" . . . We green-hands who had been expecting a visit from "Old-Nep," for some-time were looking in vain for the strange sail when we were suddenly seized and thrust into the forecastle and the door fastened. We had been in there a little while, when we heard a deep hoarse voice hail the ship, "ship a-ho-y! Halloo! Give me a rope's end for I'm coming aboard to see if you have got any of my children there." "Aye, Aye, sir!" sings out the captain, "Heave him a rope there some of you." Pretty soon we heard him and his clerk clamber over the side and get on deck. Sometime had elapsed, when we were summoned on deck to appear before his majesty, crew and all. After scanning each face he sees a face not familiar to him, he asks his name which is quickly answered by the young man; and so on with the rest. After this we were all sent back to the forecastle and fastened in again. A minute or two had passed before one of the men appeared and taking one of us blindfolded him and led him aft. The rest of us climbing up to the windows listened; and we could hear a splashing and sputtering from the victim, amid the laughing of the officers and crew. My turn came third I was blindfolded and led aft 'till I was told to step up and set down on the pig-pen; after I had sat down the barber asked my name which I had about half out when the shaving brush was shoved into my mouth (the brush was a piece of wood, with oakum wound round it, covered with tar and grease) After spitting half of the slush out of my mouth, his majesty commanded me to speak louder, which I did; this not suiting his majesty a speaking trumpet was held upto my my mouth at an angle of forty-five degrees. I had hardly got my mouth open, when a bucket full of salt-water came rusking down my throat. After this "Old Nep," put the following questions to me. "Will you swear never to walk when you can ride unless you choose to walk?" "Yes Sir" says I, and in goes the tar brush again "Will you swear never to kiss the maid when you can kiss the mistress when you should prefer the maid to the mistress?" "Yes sir" (accompanied by the brush) "Will you keep my laws as long as you live?" "Yes sir" (with brush) After this his majesty tells the barber that I ready to be shaved which he does, dousing the nasty grease and tar up my nostrils, in my mouth and ears, afterwards scraping it all off with a huge wooden razor, and wiping it with a towel 'till it is red as a beet. After shaving me "Old Nep" tells me to get up which I do thinking he is done with me; but had hardly got on my feet when a plank is quickly drawn from under and I go splash into a great hogshead of salt water up to my neck which I crawl out of like a drowned rat. The bandage is taken off now, and I shake hands with "Old Nep," as one of his sons. There was one more "greeny" which I had the pleasure of seeing go through the same ceremony. After all was done his majesty and clerk were treated to a glass of ale each; and the crew with ginger–bread for supper.

Initiation Implements.

Objects used in the Neptune ceremony were makeshift, and depended upon what was available on shipboard. In this case the god of the sea used a porpoise fork for a trident, a newspaper for his list of greenhands, and a specially crafted razor. On some ships, where such wooden razors were not to be found, greenhands were shaved with rusty iron barrel hoops.

Isaac Baker, *Tarquin*, 1862
Private Collection

The Neptune ritual aboard the *Tarquin* was performed by the ship's crew, but it was sanctioned and probably enjoyed by the shipmaster and his mates. The captains of some vessels, though, prohibited an official ceremony and sailors took the initiation into their own hands. On a few occasions, these impromptu rituals had serious consequences. On the ship *Columbus* in 1838, for example, according to journal keeper Holden Willcox, some of the crew forced a shave upon a black sailor named William Knobb. Knobb, being an experienced sailor, neither needed nor appreciated this initiation and took out his jackknife and stabbed two of his persecutors. He, then, was beaten in turn. On the ship *Elizabeth*, which crossed the line in the Pacific in April 1847, members of the crew "hooked on to the cook" and doused him with buckets of water. The cook, choosing the wrong moment for revenge, heaved a club of wood at one of the boatsteerers just as the captain emerged from his cabin. The master grabbed the cook by the throat and boxed his ears. The rest of the crew, according to diarist Thomas Bryant, escaped punishment.

Sailors had strong reasons for performing the

"Here's Luck and A Pleasant Passage."

Sailors were usually permitted a glass of grog at the close of the Neptune visit. On a few ships, this celebratory drink was deemed so crucial to the event that when the shipmaster refused to serve liquor the sailors called off the ceremony.

Isaac Baker, *Tarquin*, 1862
Private Collection

Isaac Baker, *Tarquin*, 1862
Private Collection

Exeunt Omnes.

Neptune ritual, even when the event was officially banned. First of all, on shipboard, where absolute subjection to authority was expected, the Neptune visit was a rare, legitimate opportunity for men who had no influence over others to exert some. Mariners who had relinquished the right to walk, talk, and sleep when and where they pleased—who had given up almost all the claims of free individuals—were able, on this one occasion, to exercise some power. The ceremony, then, was probably a safety valve and served, temporarily at least, to absorb some of the tensions between the crew and the afterguard.

Besides serving as an outlet for frustration and aggression, the crossing ritual served, possibly on a symbolic level only, as a puberty rite. The ceremony's emphasis on shaving and baptism in water suggests this, as does certain terminology in the event, such as the "sons" or "children" of Neptune. In addition, King Neptune gave his initiates "advice" on sexual and social behavior in the same way a father would instruct his adolescent child. Since most foremast hands were barely out of their teens, such a ritualized induction into adulthood may have been appropriate.

On many levels, then, Neptune's visit was a rite of passage. Most important of its many functions, though, according to the testimony of its perpetrators and participants, was that it signaled the admission of landsmen into the select brotherhood of sailors. Once they had crossed the line, greenhands, no matter how young, formally became "old salts."

This is Edward Haskell's own composite version of the Neptune visit aboard the *Tarquin*.

Edward Haskell, *Tarquin*, 1862
Peabody Museum of Salem

5
High Times in the Dogwatch

Here we are . . . penned up as it were in a small floating world with nothing to distract our attention or keep us in a frolicsome mood except what we make by our own exertions. But in spite of winds, passing squalls, little civil disturbances that will happen, hard work & exposure to all weather in all climates still we can yet find some sport on board. . . .

—Isaac Baker on the ship *Warsaw*, 1840

Limited by almost everything but their imaginations, deepwater sailors were adept at transforming their small ships into places of live entertainment and creative amusement. On calm nights, vessels afloat in wide, empty oceans were microcosms of activity where seamen made music, danced, spun yarns, and played games. The time for the fun was usually the second dogwatch, from six to eight in the evening, and the hub of activity was always the forecastle.

When sailors had enough stamina, which was almost any night without a gale, they played music. It was a rare ship that did not carry a seaman who could perform on the flute, fiddle, or accordion, or at least a man who was willing to improvise on pots, pans, funnels, or bones. While much forecastle music was nothing more than spontaneous racket, some was formally organized, and a few sailors even had the wit and energy to organize full concerts. On the *Lucy Ann*, for instance, the crew performed a complete musical revue for an audience of seagulls in February 1842. The program, which was copied down by crew member John Martin, included a wide variety of choral pieces and instrumental duets. Early in the show, a sailor

nicknamed "Hominy head" entertained his shipmates with a song called "I hit her right on her stinking machine." Hominy head was followed by Martin himself, who played a solo on his bugle, and then by the steward, who sang "My Dogs eyes makes mince pies." After a series of solos, the last part of the performance began with a song by "Mocho a color'd gentleman" entitled "So early in the morning the Sailors love the bottle O." After a few more choral works, a stern order from the aftercabin forced the festival to an abrupt close. The production "wound up," wrote Martin, "by the Mate telling us if we did not quit making such a damned noise, he would heave a bucket of stinking water over us."

In contrast to the *Lucy Ann*'s first officer, the mate of the *Warsaw*, Isaac Baker, took pride in describing his vessel's musical efforts. He noted in 1840 that the ship's glee club was so well-organized that its members had developed a set of by-laws. These included a rule that anyone who disturbed glee club performances had to "sing five good songs in succession or recieve nineteen pinches from each member while saying the law," and another that "All spectators who are in the hall (or forcastle as the vulgar call it) must stay & all passers up & down during the performance of anything must forfeit a cigar, chew of tobacco, or else sing a song."

Given the range of equipment on each vessel and, still more, the diversity of sailors' tastes and talents, shipboard music was often wildly eclectic. The clash of musical styles produced on the whaleship *Eliza Adams* one night in January 1852 demonstrates the variety of sounds one ship could generate. "Went forward to night to hear some music," wrote John Jones, a cook on the vessel.

. . . found the fidler playing the fourth of July Evans keeping time with the bones, the blacksmith playing Juber on the banjo, Goss was playing Bonapart crossing the alps on the fife, and Kimble was whistling Yankee Dodle Do—the Portugues was singing a song of their own, and some of the rest was singing old Dan Tucker is come to town, came aft as far as the stearage found the fiddle there and accordian in full blast, one singing when I can read my title clear, another O Miss Lucy Neal—then went into the Cabin and found the old man rattlin away at the Symnocope the rest trying verry hard to go to sleep, then laid down on a chest thought of the girl I left behind me fel asleep and dreamt of thunder. . . .

Not infrequently, forecastle music led to forecastle dancing, and in good weather seamen went out onto the deck or into the ship's waist to shuffle and stamp together. Not discouraged by the absence of women, sailors on several vessels fabricated female partners with costumes. On the *Atkins Adams,* for instance, sailors used feather pillows and a nightgown to create a dancing partner named "Molly" for the hornpipe. And at a dance on the ship *Montreal,* which took place at twilight in January 1852, an entire watch came up on deck in their "draws," impersonating ladies. According to the steward, Washington Fosdick, this complete set of men and "women" then had a fore and after, with a "regular, old fashioned 'break down' 'drag out' 'double shuffle' which made up in energy what it lacked in grace, sounding very much like a locomotive at full speed over a rickety track where the rails were all loose."

Sailors who grew tired of dancing or who had performed one musical revue too many invented other kinds of revelry. On several vessels foremast hands formed themselves into militia troops and, using broomsticks and mop handles, maneuvered in formation around the decks. Other seamen devised original pranks and games. On the *Atkins Adams* sailors regularly played "whang O doodle" after sundown. In this game, according to participant William Abbe, crewmen chased each other around the windlass, spanking rear ends as they ran: "fast & terrible are some of the blows—and we are kept in a roar of laughter—at the contorted faces— and the rubbing with hands of the wounded parts." Similar hijinks were reported on the *Esquimaux* by the ship's cooper, J. B. Hersey. Hersey, twenty-three, noted with distant amusement the revels of the forecastle hands, all boys aged sixteen to nineteen. Hersey was particularly impressed by their pubescent behavior one May night in 1843, when they began to imitate poultry. The Indian cakes that they had had for supper, claimed the cooper, afforded them "a

fine opportunity for indulging in their propensities for merriment."

Several of the crew could be seen with some of the meal in their mouths fluttering about deck striking their hands against their sides to resemble the wings of a fowl accompanied with crowing, cackling and gaging in imitation of a hen half shocked. From the various sounds which salutes ones ear he would naturally be led to infer that he was within the prescribed limits of a country poultry yard. . . .

Foremast hands did not, of course, spend every night in noisy, physical frolics. In cold or inclement weather they often passed the dogwatch or their time off duty enjoying quiet pastimes like reading or playing cards. Others found entertainment in storytelling. In fact, spinning yarns probably served, more than any other activity, to while away long, tedious hours. One of the few diarists to take the time to record stories was John Martin, who apparently had nothing better to do on a stormy night in 1842 than to recount three tales he had just heard. With their elements of exaggeration and their reliance on superstition, they fit the classic description of a "yarn."

The first tale was by a boatsteerer, who entertained his listeners with a short story about one of his former voyages around Cape Horn. On this particular trip, he explained,

all hands agreed to let their beards grow until their arrival home partly out of a joke & partly to strain their coffee through, the Cockroaches being so thick on board as soon as it was passed below it was half filled with them. one of their beards grew to such a length it reached to his knees & a Barber in New Bedford offered him $5 to let him shave him as he wanted his beard for a sign.

After a yarn by the same man about an albacore which had caught eighty-one flying fish, the cook told a ghost story about an apparition one of his shipmates had seen on his last voyage. "In the evening," Martin records the cook as saying,

when the watch went below to turn in he thought he saw something white flitting about his bunk of a strange unearthly appearance & called the attention of his watch mates to it, but they saw nothing. one of the oldest hands remarked to another that something

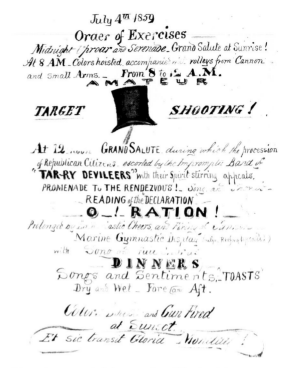

WARSAW THEATRE.

Benefit of Mr BACON.

This Evening (June 27th) will be

shown, a true specimen of

Mr BACON'S VOCAL POWERS.

Part 1st Sally of Our Alley A Solo — Mr Bacon

Naval Songs — Messrs Barron & Bacon.

Part 2nd Several new Comic Songs written

at Mr BACON'S request and sung

by him in character.

Part 3d The whole to conclude with a

FAMOUS SONG beginning with

"There was a Little Man."

Chorus — With a High Jig Jig & a Low Jig Jig &c.

Performances to commence at 6½ o'clock.

Tickets Gratis! Children half price!!

A playbill from the ship *Warsaw* testifies to the skill with which sailors stretched limited human resources to their utmost creative potential.

Isaac Baker, *Warsaw*, 1840

Private Collection

Accordion

This accordion is said to have been used by sailors aboard a Salem vessel in the African trade, around 1850.

July 4th 1859

Order of Exercises —

Midnight Uproar and Serenade — Grand Salute at Sunrise!

At 8 AM — Colors hoisted, accompanied with volleys from Cannon

and small Arms. — From 8 to 9 A.M.

AMATEUR

TARGET   SHOOTING !

At 12 noon. GRAND SALUTE *during which the procession*

of Republican Citizens, escorted by the Impromptu Band of

TAR-RY DEVILEERS with their Spirit stirring appeals,

PROMENADE To THE RENDEZVOUS! — Song at ——

READING of the DECLARATION

O —! RATION !

Prolonged by Enthusiastic Cheers and Firing of Cannon —

Marine Gymnastic Display —

with Song of True ——

DINNERS

Songs and Sentiments, TOASTS

Dry and Wet — Fore and Aft.

Colors down and Gun Fired

at Sunset.

Et sic transit Gloria Mundi !

Many American holidays, such as Thanksgiving or Christmas, were ignored at sea, but sailors usually did their best to celebrate the Fourth of July. Mustering whatever firearms they could, they marched on deck, fired guns into space, and made as much noise as the shipmaster would allow.

Isaac Baker, *Golconda*, 1859

Private Collection

Scrimshaw Tooth and Book

Scrimshanders sometimes drew not only their inspiration but also their exact designs from popular publications. In this case, the whaleman used the cover illustration from *Fanny Campbell: Female Pirate Captain* by "Lieutenant Murray." He probably relied on a pin-prick technique to copy the drawing. With this method he would have positioned the illustration over the tooth so that he could push a small pin through the outlines of the design into the tooth itself. He would then have connected the dots to form a continuous line and filled the design in with black ink.

serious would happen to him before long, he was the Carpenter. in the morning they were called to take in sail as it was blowing quite fresh. The Carpenter laid out on the Fore Topsail yard to help reef the sail when it knocked him off into the sea. the ship was immediately hove aback & a boat lowered but a heavy Sea running at the time nearly filled it when it was called back the Captain thinking it was better to lose one man than to risk the lives of half a dozen, so the poor Carpenter sank to rise no more.

The *Lucy Ann* began to "ship so many seas herself" just then that the cook's story was the last the sailors heard before being called to tend their own sails in the storm outside.

While the dogwatch was often enjoyed communally, sailors used this time for individual projects as well, such as writing in journals and working on crafts. The numbers of carved models, ropework objects, and scrimshaw that have survived testify to the importance of decorative arts as a preoccupation of off-duty seamen. Sailors also spent considerable energy during the dogwatch and on Sundays repairing and patching their personal belongings. "Started the sewing society again," reported Robert Weir on the *Clara Bell* in 1856, "stitch on stitch, patch on patch is all the rage—here are half the ship crew below—going it hammer & tonge with their needles." "To look into our Forecastle this afternoon one would think it was a Tailor's shop," echoed seaman Henry Davis in 1862, "for one is making Pants another Shirts another is puzzling his brains over a Cap and the last Knight of the Needle is mending."

On the ship *Illinois,* the foremast hands even held a quilting bee. "One of our fellows quilt wanted quilting," noted Elias Trotter on December 3, 1846: "He got 4 Iron poles for a frame & adjusting it in rather an odd manner, called upon his watch for assistance. The jacks both old & small, brought their needles & their palms & sitting around on chests & buckets & barges surrounded the quilting by the number of ten." The *Illinois* sailors completed the entire piece in one watch and ended the effort with dances and songs.

In the aftercabin, officers with time to kill usually found their diversions alone. They read to themselves, wrote letters home, or played their fiddles and accordions to imaginary com-

Model in Bottle

In addition to producing ships in bottles, seamen were adept at inserting other objects into bottles by mysterious means. While some parts of the toy saw and trestle here were apparently collapsed, then placed in the bottle and pulled open with strings, it is not apparent how the cross piece on the stopper was inserted.

pany. For some of these men, the chance to have private, quiet moments was a pleasure. For others, though, life in the aftercabin was isolated and lonely. "Here I set in my state room," lamented mate Benjamin Boodry on the *Arnolda* in 1853, "the door shut and my whole family of Daguerrotypes around me and my Accordion in my hand and try to immagine myself in Mattapoisett." Protocol prevented officers like Boodry from conversing too freely with shipmasters. And shipmasters, for their part, frequently found lesser officers unsuitable company. Captain D. F. Weekes on the bark *Brothers,* for instance, felt especially downhearted on a Sunday in March 1866 because he was "agraveted," as he put it, by having no one to talk with. "The mate is young and boyish all his thoughts is light and unstable," he complained, "& the 2d mate I do not like to make free to talk with as I think it would not do so well."

Preferring the company of their own kind, merchant shipmasters often had to wait for a port stop before they could relax with senior officers. Even though they were able to visit other masters while both were under sail, these men were usually too much in a hurry at sea to exchange anything but signals. And even the signals were occasionally omitted by a sea captain bent on a fast passage. On the ship *Merrimac,* for example, mate Isaac Baker noted with disappointment the businesslike manner of his captain when he refused to acknowledge a bark that was passing them close by. "It *does* seem kind of unneighborly," wrote Baker, "to pass a fellow and not say How d'ye do? Get out of my way or something of the kind besides twon't do the flags any harm to air them occasionally. . . ."

No one knew better about the unfriendliness of a merchant ship than a whaler. Whalemen, who not only signaled ships regularly but exchanged evening visits as a matter of course on cruising grounds, were often rebuked by merchantmen who did not want to stop and chat. Not infrequently, a whaler wanting to meet for a "gam," as ocean meetings were called, hauled her main yard back as a signal for a visit, only to be ignored by a fast-moving merchant ship. A journal entry by John Randall on the ship *California* in November 1849 describes a typical social encounter between a whaler and a trading vessel:

. . . saw a sail off our starboard bow she prooved to be a large Merchant man we hove our yard aback but she passed us to big to speak with us Blubber Hunters we braced the yards and stood on.

Whalers had far better luck socializing with their own kind. Indeed, whaleships on poor hunting grounds often spent more time engaged in gams than they did looking for their prey. Their need for outside social contact after months of isolation was sometimes quite desperate and, as a young sailor named John Spooner explained in 1862, the sight of a

Beckets

The rope handles of a sea chest, known as beckets, were often decorated with paint or carved wood. In this case, the turk's head knots are painted red, white, and blue. The weave in these beckets is a simple braid.

friendly sail on the horizon was often cause for celebration:

. . . none but a sailor . . . can tell the emotions which are excited by those too simple and apparently meaningless words "Sail Oh" But if a few of or any one who may happen to read this page should be "forty three" days and not see any signs of human beings but those who are in that little world called a ship, I think they would understand fully the meaning of those two simple words "Sail oh."

During the gam itself, boats plied between visiting ships with sailors of every rank, who set about social mixing with abandon. Officers congregated in the aftercabin to show off daguerreotypes and to share liquor; boatsteerers held forth in the steerage, and seamen gossiped together in the forecastle. As Silliman Ives, steward on the *Sunbeam,* explained, a whaleman's gam resembled a "tea party" more than anything else:

Every one gets up their "fan tackle," and then they go at it, and the way small talk suffers is a caution.

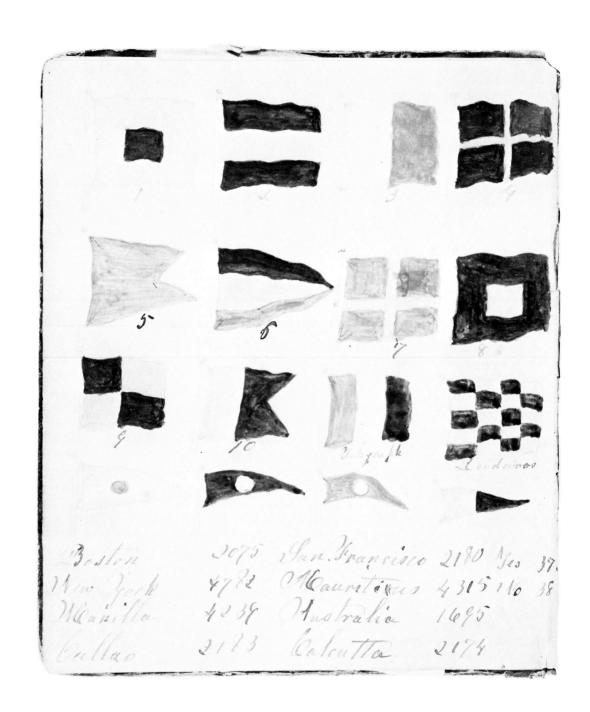

Boston   3075   San Francisco   2180   Yes   37

New York   4782   Mauritius   4315   No   38

Manilla   4038   Australia   1695

Callao   3183   Calcutta   2174

All the news that has lately been heard, and considerable more that is manufactured on the spur of the moment, is exchanged. The whales that have been caught on the voyage, all have to be caught, and killed over again, and some that were captured on previous voyages have to suffer a further slaughter, it maybe for the twentieth time. The yield from such fares doesn't amount to much however. Officers are talked of and about, and their various merits, or demerits discussed. And in many instances, the "dis" is dispensed with. And so the many tongues wag merrily for the space of three, or four hours when the command of "man the boat" puts an end to the visit. At such times an exchange of reading matter takes place, and many's the old acquaintance that one meets in this way during the voyage. . . . These little breaks in our monotonous existence are very pleasant, and furnish us with material for thought as well as serving to stir us up a bit, so that we may not stagnate altogether.

Whaleships were so successful at gamming that a number of sailors actually grew tired of deepwater society. J. E. Haviland, a sailor on the *Baltic,* complained in July 1857 that he was "getting sick" of gamming. "It is impossible to get any sleep," he declared, "when you have a boats crew gaming in the forecastle." Other sailors were annoyed, not by gamming in general, but by particular ships that they had seen too frequently. "Spoke that Confounded Ship again the Lion i wish to the Lord She was somewhere else," wrote Sylvanus Tallman of the *Canada* in 1848. Silliman Ives, who had enjoyed the company of the *Kathleen* in January 1870, found that after a year of her close attendance he not only wished her completely out of his sight, but

also decided that if he ever had a friend of that name, he'd cut her acquaintance. His master, he concluded, was all too fond of the other ship: ". . . he is wild if he loses sight of her for an hour, and if he should go a week without seeing her, he would be a fit candidate for a straight jacket. Now the 'Kathleen's' people are all nice folks for all that I know to the contrary. But there is such a thing as having a surfiet of good things and I'm sure I'm stuffed full of 'Kathleen' as ever I was of roast turkey and mince pie on a Thanksgiving Day. And I <u>know</u> I don't want to see her anymore."

For the most part, though, sailors welcomed the presence of friendly ships. If nothing else, visiting other vessels showed some men that their own forecastles were not half as bad as they thought they were. William Abbe, for example, found that the *Sea Queen*, a bark he went aboard in June 1859, was dark, dreary, and oppressive: "They have prayers every morning aboard this bark—her skipper officiating as chaplain—no noise of singing or dancing or music is allowed—no loud conversation permitted—the crew are debarred almost every resource a sailor has to relieve the monotony & tedium of a voyage."

In contrast to the *Sea Queen*, Abbe's own ship, the *Atkins Adams*, was full of merriment and frolic. On the same night that he discovered the sorrowful bark, the *Atkins Adams* held a moonlight dance with two other vessels. Its success so impressed Abbe that he gave the event special space, not to mention eloquence, in his diary:

The 3 barks lay nearly in a triangle—on a quiet sea—in nearly a dead calm—while the moon . . . shed a brilliant light over the ocean—& shone with elfish gleam on the white sails of the 3 ships—We could see in the distance two other ships gamming—& amidst this scene of quiet beauty—beneath the moon—joining with the new boats crew we danced away. sanding the decks & kicking off our shoes as we formed two cotillion parties & kept the decks alive—crowded as they were—with our shouts & laughter & music.

Nights like these, when the dogwatch stretched on to midnight and ships' crews came together in spontaneous camaraderie, were for Abbe and other sailors like him, some of the happiest moments of seafaring life.

A shipmaster who was in too much of a hurry to gam or to speak with another vessel could always "signalize" her. By hoisting combinations of numbered or lettered flags or pennants, vessels exchanged longitude, ports of departure and destination, and length of time out. If they wished to, they could extend the conversation. By using a code book of signals, they could say anything from "our owner is bankrupt" to "a man has fallen overboard." The flags in Edward Haskell's drawing are those presented in Captain Marryat's "universal" code of signals, which was widely used throughout the nineteenth century.

Edward Haskell, *Tarquin,* 1862
Peabody Museum of Salem

6
Liberty Days

Land oh! oh!! oh!!! oh!!!!

—John Spooner on the *Mt. Wollaston,* September 16, 1862

From his first sweet scent of a land breeze to his last heave on a windlass as his ship weighed anchor, the sailor's visit to shore was a fast-paced adventure. Liberty days were well-named, for the man who rowed into port after a long sea voyage acted like no one so much as a released prisoner.

These diaries suggest that sailors on shore leave had two tasks—to make up for past deprivations and to stockpile experiences for the future. What they missed most at sea, of course, were women, alcohol, and fresh food, and the order in which these needs were fulfilled depended on the particular appetites of the men involved.

If it was the opposite sex they sought most eagerly, many sailors did not even have to wait to find brothels ashore. In remote ports of the world, particularly in the islands of the Pacific or Indian Oceans, native women and men, sometimes in droves, swam or rowed out to visiting ships. The women had much to sell. They offered sailors fresh fruit, vegetables, hogs, chickens, and tourist items of native manufacture. Many also hoped to sell sexual favors.

The process of soliciting or procuring sex varied from ship to ship. On the bark *Doctor Franklin,* which sailed into St. Helena harbor in March 1857, women who came from shore to wash sailors' clothes indicated with special subtlety that they were not only laundresses but prostitutes as well. Diarist Dan Whitfield reported that these washerwomen, who were "Fine Rosy cheeked Buxom Looking Lasses, . . . as full of deviltry as an egg is full of meat,"

told the men that "they did not depend altogether upon the washing they got for A Livelihood. But, that very often they Picked up A sweetheart when they came off to ships. . . ."

How long women stayed aboard and under what conditions was usually up to the ship's first officer, who was in charge of the vessel during a port stay. Some mates were probably like Ambrose Bates on the *Nimrod,* who was so "sick to death" of women coming alongside his ship that he forbade female visitations. At the other end of the spectrum was the *Doctor Franklin*'s mate, who not only permitted women and liquor aboard but helped turn his vessel into a floating drunken brothel. According to Dan Whitfield,

Isaac Baker was so struck by the formidable limbs and dress of his stewardess aboard the *Golconda* that he composed a poem describing the success with which she blocked the sunlight in the aftercabin. The poem ended as follows:

> The Stewardess! (Oh, bless her limbs
> Th'Effect indeed is risible)
> Descending slowly causes now
>   A "Total Eclipse"!
>   Thus Visible!

Isaac Baker, *Golconda,* 1859

Private Collection

the *Doctor Franklin,* while in port at St. Helena in 1859, was the home of "drunken sailors and drunken whores." "We have Not got a Sober officer belonging to her," commented the sailor, "and in fact sober Men of any grade is A Scarce Article in the Bark Doctor Franklin."

The sailors and the women aboard this ship were so inebriated, in fact, that they could barely even muster the strength to dance or sing. As Whitfield explained:

Reels, Jigs, Country Dances, Cotileons, Waltzes, and Polkas were all tried successively & there was some very good dancers among the women. They kept it up until 10 O clock, when the Fidler being too drunk to Play any More, they commenced singing But, some of the girls having used the Glass Pretty freely, the Songs, . . . so affected them that most of them were soon in tears & were escorted to bed by those of the Male Gender who were in A condition to help them.

"The Bay of Islands is one of the most beautiful Bays in the world," exulted a seaman on the *Julian* in 1848. Here, at least seven American vessels have anchored in this New Zealand location.

Joseph Ray, *Edward Cary,* 1854
Nantucket Historical Association

And where was the mate, the commanding officer? "The Old Mate," claimed Whitfield, was "sprawled out on the Cabin Floor with Nothing but his shirt on his Nakedness exposed to everyone. . . ."

For all their rowdiness, the liaisons between sailors and their prostitutes do not seem to have been simply loose associations. Many of the seamen who confessed to shore attachments visited or entertained only one woman while they were in port and frequently referred to these companions as their "wives." In many ways sailors seemed to try to replicate the kind of monogamous relationship that they might have wanted or enjoyed at home. On the whaleship *Ann Perry,* for example, sailors were so eager for female loyalty that they paid their shore partners to be faithful to them. As seaman Ezra Goodnough remarked in July 1847:

. . . we must get some oil or I shall not be able to get my girl in Mahe [Africa] a new dress when i get back there, if i do not get her a dress she will forget me you see we can hire the girls in Mahe to remember us that is more than the girls at home will do they will not think of a poor Devil either for love or money out of sight out of mind or at least it appears so . . .

This portrait of a sailor with patched clothes, bare toes, and a red nose, describes any number of seamen after a long cruise and a brief interlude on liberty. Why this man is carrying a shovel is not evident.

Anonymous, *Orray Taft,* c. 1864
Kendall Whaling Museum

On shore at the Bay of Islands, New Zealand, a sailor, possibly the author himself, rests beneath a well-visited flagstaff on a hill overlooking one of the harbors.

Anonymous, *Sea Ranger,* n. d.
Kendall Whaling Museum

Possibly expressing a similar need for commitment, several sailors on the ship *Columbus,* which visited the Bay of Islands in 1838, decided to marry their women. When the ship left port, of course, the marriages had to be annulled. But, as a sailor named Holden Willcox explained, the separation came easily to all parties: ". . . all our young men what had got married since our arrival here, got divorced by mutual consent and their late spouses with all their children and donnage either went on shore or on board of some other ships to obtain new employement."

For the pleasures of their company, women were compensated in various ways. Many traded their favors for money, others for calico, clothing, tobacco, or pipes. Some women were prohibited from personally accepting any goods or money by their brothers or fathers who, according to native social custom, managed their prostitution and accepted payment for them. This practice was reported frequently by sailor diarists who visited New Zealand. Orson Shattuck, a seaman on the *Frances,* was shocked by the system of prostitution he saw there in 1851, by which "miserable and unfortunate little girls" were compelled by their relatives "to give themselves up to our rugh and brutal sailors."

While some seamen could take their shore pleasures on their ships, most others had to indulge their desires on land. Sailors were usually allowed liberty with the rest of their watch and went ashore anywhere from a few hours to a day and a night. Shipmasters often advanced crewmen money, up to $1.00 a day, which came out of their wages or lay. This money was never enough, of course, and seamen went on shore with numerous schemes for making more. On the *Lucy Ann* in 1842, for instance, sailors who headed ashore at St. Iago were ready for hard bargaining. As John Martin reported:

[we] were all rigged from stem to stern in [our] best, with a supply of Tobacco; side combs, & handkerchiefs to trade for fruit & other articles unnecessary to mention. we all had ourselves bolstered up with

---

Anonymous, *Orray Taft,* c. 1864
Kendall Whaling Museum

"Went ashore this morning. And the first place I steered for was the market for I longed to get a bite from a peach again," wrote sailor Robert Weir as he landed in St. Helena in 1858. Another sailor, J. E. Haviland, complained after a fruit eating binge in Lahaina in 1856, "I have eaten so much I expect it will make me sick." Similarly attracted to fruit markets was the artist here, who made a watercolor sketch of the various citrus fruits for sale at Fayal in the Azores.

Anonymous, *Sea Ranger*, n. d.

Kendall Whaling Museum

tobacco, but found when getting on shore it was unnecessary to keep it concealed, as the officers made no search. as soon as the boat touched the beach we were surrounded by the Portuguese white yellow & black, with you have tobacco, I have orange you trade me I trade you. but we forced our way through them up a hill. . . .

How a sailor spent his liberty days depended not only on his own disposition but also on native laws and customs. Sailors who wanted to drink at Lahaina in the Sandwich Islands in 1846, for instance, were out of luck because, according to John Aiken on the ship *Virginia*, Lahaina was a temperance port. It was the "still and quietest place" Aiken had ever seen, with "400 men going on shore on liberty every day and they have to come off sober." Ten years later, J. E. Haviland, a foremast hand on the bark *Baltic*, found it easy enough to buy liquor at Lahaina but hard to stay in port long enough to enjoy it—on certain nights a drum beat at seven o'clock, and all men without special passes from the harbormaster had to return to their vessels or risk imprisonment.

Local laws on some islands prohibited women from visiting ships, and on others limited prostitution even on land. A sailor named Thomas Morrison, who was visiting McAskills Island in the Pacific, claimed that missionaries had some influence over the latter situation. "I and some others," Morrison noted on March 13, 1873, "went on shore with great expectations but got greatly disapointed the Missionarys has got glory pumped into the natives good and at both ends."

It was not the intention of every seaman to spend all of his days in port in one long, libidinous frolic. Many sailors passed their holiday enjoying the simple pastime of getting exercise, and rambled about foreign countrysides on foot or by horse. "The height of a sailor's ambition is arrived at when he can get command of a horse,"

In this fanciful watercolor of King Neptune and a "Neptress," the monarchs are pulled through the water in chariots by horses with whales' tails. The significance of the "Old Cove" is unclear.

Abraham Gardner?, *Canton*, 1834–38

Kendall Whaling Museum

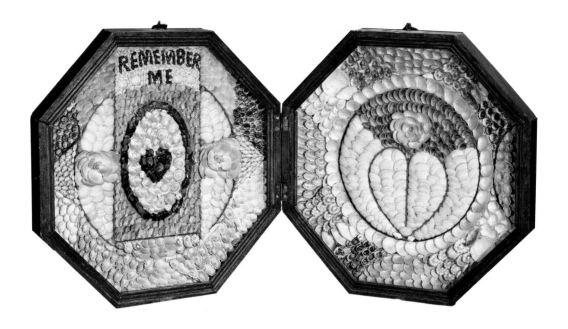

Sailor's Valentine

Popular souvenir items among sailors were these valentines, long thought to have been produced on shipboard. Most of these boxes, which contain intricate shellwork designs, were manufactured for visiting mariners on the islands of Barbados and Grenadine in the West Indies in the nineteenth century.

Courtesy of Mr. and Mrs. Robert Storer.

Captain Frederick H. Smith, *Petrel,* 1873

Kendall Whaling Museum

Joseph Ray, *Edward Cary*, 1854
Nantucket Historical Association

claimed Silliman Ives in 1869, and other diarists concurred that an afternoon galloping around the outskirts of a town or at breakneck speed through a native village was a liberty day well spent. ". . . if we do not fall off more than once in a quarter of a mile we mak tolerable fair weather of it the Natives appear to be amused at our sports & seem anxious to help us to the worst horses they can find," reported rider John Randall from the bark *Cleora* in the Celebes in 1853.

Visiting foreign markets was another popular liberty activity for sailors. Provision-deprived seamen went into ecstasies over local fruits and vegetables and shopped for souvenirs like sample pepper bags, carved boxes, weapons, shawls, and birds and monkeys. They were also enthusiastic about excursions and tried to see as much of the foreign world as their money or energy would allow. Sailors to the southern hemisphere had favorite tourist spots. Captain Cook's burial place was a must for seamen who visited the Sandwich Islands; Napoleon's tomb was the highlight of St. Helena; and Juan Fernandez, Robinson Crusoe's island, was a necessary stop for newcomers to the eastern Pacific Ocean.

Jaded seamen who had already seen the standard spots of interest found other ways to amuse themselves on shore. In more populated ports, sailors visited billiard halls and gambling rooms, and those who sought more sedate forms of diversion went to local reading rooms, to missionaries' houses, or to the consul's office. Shipmasters, who usually spent their days on shore in boarding houses, passed their time calling on local government officials and participating in dinners, teas, and dances.

Although the fact runs counter to their popular reputations, a large number of seamen actually attended church during port stops. Whether they visited halls of worship out of honest religious conviction, or from a desire to please an evangelistic shipmaster, or simply to get a close look at some of the native population is not clear. At least one ship's crew managed to combine churchgoing with another favorite shore activity. As John Martin of the *Lucy Ann* reported in July 1842, "the Starboard watch went on shore to day on liberty, some of the

Sailors did not usually succeed in their attempts to desert ship, largely because their shipmasters offered rewards for their capture. Here, four men, including the cook, have taken "French leave" from the whaleship *Elizabeth,* and the master is offering $4.00 for their apprehension.

Peleg Lawrence, *Elizabeth,* 1849
Peabody Museum of Salem

crew went to church. Mr. Sherritt the Storekeeper preached. after church was out he opened his store & sold grog to the sailors."

Shipmasters naturally hoped that sailors would return to their vessels after their holidays ready and willing to weigh anchor for another passage. Seamen were rarely eager to set sail with the same group of men, however, and many hoped to use their liberty days as a chance to leave one ship and sign on to another. But wishing to leave a ship and successfully accomplishing a discharge or desertion were very different things. Merchant seamen, who remained in large ports for sometimes several months at a time, frequently had no difficulty securing official discharges. Their shipmasters often used shore labor to handle cargo and then signed new men on for the next voyage. Whaling captains, on the other hand, visited remote harbors where substitute seamen were not available, and they did their best to hang on to their original crews. On occasion they attempted to give their men

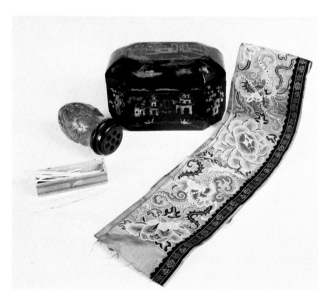

Fijian Eating Fork

A wooden eating fork like this nineteenth century example would have been used by Fijian priests and chiefs for consuming human flesh. These high officials were prohibited by "tapu" (taboo) from touching any meat with their hands. Sailors were endlessly fascinated by cultures which practiced cannibalism.

Human Hair Necklace

If a sailor visiting the Sandwich Islands had nails, tobacco, or cloth to trade, he could probably have obtained a human hair necklace like the one pictured above. These necklaces, which held a hook of either whale or walrus ivory, were traditionally worn by native men and women of high rank. The hair is braided, with approximately fifty to ninety hairs per braid. Several hundred of these braids make up a necklace. During the mid to late nineteenth century, Hawaiians served as crew on whaling vessels and brought back whale teeth and walrus tusks to be made into hooks.

Souvenirs from China

Sailors ashore at well-established ports like Hong Kong, Canton, Manila, or Melbourne, spent their souvenir money on items mass-produced for tourists. All the items shown here were manufactured in China. The cricket cage, on the left, was made from a gourd grown in a ceramic mold. It housed crickets, which the Chinese used for fighting contests and kept as pets. The ivory jackstraws (pick-up-sticks) and the lacquered tea caddy were specifically manufactured in China for trade with the West. The embroidered silk panels, on the other hand, were probably made for native use, as they were normally attached to the sleeve of a Chinese embroidered coat.

Parrot in Whalebone Cage

Many sailors were incurable souvenir hunters, and before their passage back to America purchased foreign animals for pets or presents. Most of these animals escaped or died before they reached America, but some completed the voyage, like this African Gray Parrot. The parrot is housed here in a dome-topped whalebone cage.

liberty in places so desolate that potential deserters would be discouraged.

Even when whaleships did visit more cosmopolitan ports, whaling shipmasters tried to make arrangements with local officials to have natives bring back deserting sailors for a fee charged, of course, to the seaman's account. The natives of Lahaina were so eager to arrest deserters that sailors, even on their best behavior, had trouble avoiding the "calaboose," or jail. William Stetson, on shore leave from the *Arab*, reported that he could barely go for a walk in the town in September 1856 without being followed by "kanakas," or natives, ready to arrest him for suspected desertion. Stetson fell into their eager hands when he unintentionally walked "too far" and he spent the night in jail.

There were really very few alternatives for those sailors who deserted successfully. Some were destined to become permanent vagrants in foreign countries. These "drifters," or "beachcombers" as sailors called them, were the objects of considerable scorn. Active sailors condemned them for their indolence and dissipation and, according to John Martin, who encountered a large group of these white expatriates in the Pacific on February 19, 1843, even natives viewed them with disgust. "When a ship comes in," explained Martin,

the white men flock on board they are called beach combers & a regular set of scoundrels they are. they are too lazy too work at home for a living & prefer staying here where the living grows to their hands without having to work for it. their object in coming to the ship was to beg clothes as they can not go naked like the natives their skin will not stand the sun, they begged shirts, old trousers patches and took articles that the natives would not touch with one of their spears.

How many nineteenth-century sailors, American or other, became permanent drifters is hard to know. William Abbe on the *Atkins Adams* in 1859 claimed to have seen hundreds of such destitute men on the South American coast. His diary, though, is not alone in suggesting that most deserting American sailors who maintained their health eventually found jobs on ships that sailed for home. As paradisical as life in a foreign port seemed to a sailor at first, in

Native of Samoa

American sailors were intrigued by the aboriginal inhabitants of the southern hemisphere. They generally viewed them with disdain, commenting on their lack of industriousness or the "savage" nature of their customs. F. Cady's description of the natives of New Zealand is typical. "They are," he wrote, "stout robust treacherous voracious gluttinous naked set of wretches regular Yankees for trade."

Edward Haskell, *Tarquin,* 1862
Peabody Museum of Salem

---

fact, by the end of a long shore visit many seamen were relieved to be on deep water again. A foremast hand on the *Julian* spoke for several others when he indicated how happy he was to be leaving a harbor after an extenuated port stay: "as it is said," wrote F. Cady in February 1848, "a sailor is glad twice I think it was true in this instance I am sure I was that is when we entered the Bay and when we left Cape behind bound out to sea."

Edwin Pulver, who was discharged from the ship *Columbus* in 1852, eventually developed a similar distaste for shore. Pulver's main problem was his foreignness: "This Evening I feel verry lonesome," he wrote on November 24,

I am all Alone there is severl Natives Sitting at my door talking what is the topic of there conversation is more than I can tell But I all most wish I was one of them they know No troubble that is much more than I can say If A man wants to know troubble all he has to do is to be set Ashore in A foreing country without money and without friends.

Loneliness and cultural isolation like Pulver's were not the only difficulties of liberty days. By the end of a long, intense spate of freedom, most sailors were very literally sick of shore. The most energetic and pugnacious of them carried back to sea a variety of scars and illnesses. Those that did not have broken noses or black eyes as a result of brawls suffered either from alcohol withdrawal or from venereal diseases. "Ladies fever," as sailors called gonorrhea and syphilis, was a common consequence of sexual encounters, and these diseases occasionally incapacitated many of a ship's crew. On the ship *Cavalier,* for example, a number of sailors who had been entertained by Ascension Island women were forced to pay a serious price for their pleasures. "There is now more than half our men sick," reported a *Cavalier* seaman named William Wilson in 1850, "most of them with syphilis—blind bulboes abundant—It appears as if the Ladies fever had been inocculated into the larboard watch—the Mate is but a shell, a mere wreck and most of his men are diseased."

For many sailors, then, the ocean passage after a port stay was a time for recuperation. It was a time, also, for talk of beginnings—for optimism about successful voyages, fast passages, and friendly weather. With new combinations of crews and shipmasters, new supplies, and rejuvenated spirits, mariners leaving port sailed, in essence, on maiden voyages. Many echoed the sentiments of J. E. Haviland who wrote, after he had left the Sandwich Islands on the bark *Baltic* in 1856, "I feel like a new man again."

7
The Art of Journal Keeping

Wed 28 What shall I write about how can I
write anything this must be an interesting
book for anyone to read I cant write Give it up
Sept 29 Here I am trying it again tonight
my subject is this a cloudy day, in a whaleship, everything going on nicely, made sail
in the morning and took it in at night now
if anybody can make anything out of that to
interest I would like to read it.

—James Allen on the bark *Alfred Gibbs,*
September 1870

As seaman James Allen discovered, journal writing was no easy job. Had he decided to try to
keep a log, he might not have been so discouraged, for even though a log demanded technical
information, such as sail changes and ship's position, at least its author knew what words and
numbers were expected of him. "The main point
in the material of a ships Log," explained mate
Isaac Baker in 1855, is "wind and weather con-
trasted with weather and wind, a strange sail a
discovery of some broken & barnacle[d] spar,
such as we passed today and the Latitude and
Longitude." In contrast, a journal or diary demanded imaginative energy for it could be anything a sailor chose. Third mate Marshall Keith,
for instance, used his to record his dreams about
hometown girls; Captain Edward Harrington
turned his diary into a chart of his feelings,
health, and daily disposition and entitled it the
"Daily Index of My Being and Existence." Other
seamen kept their journals as books of poetry
and songs. Most journals that survive, however,
are chronological accounts of voyages, flavored
by personal opinion and introspection. And they
were kept, in part, because of the lack of anything better to do. Horace Putnam's reasons for
writing a diary on the *William Schroder* were
typical of others: "I do not intend to give all the
minute particulars that . . . happen during the
voyage but a brief outline of the events as they
may chance to occur, and as I feel disposed to
note them. I only do this for my own amusement
to pass time that might be otherwise foolishly
spent."

The journal subjects that sailors like Putnam
found to "pass time" were often ordinary events
and everyday objects that any self-respecting
shore-based writer would have considered too
prosaic. Isaac Baker, for instance, noted the
daily activities of his pet cat, Tom, wrote poetry
about his hat and jacket, and devoted space to
a comparison between ships' rigging and
women's clothing. Other seafaring authors described their shipmates, their living spaces, and
the contents of their sea chests.

By far the most popular subject for sailors'
documentation was the marine world. Even
though a few seamen dismissed the ocean as a
wide, desolate waste, others found it teeming
with inspiration. Sharks and albatrosses were
favorite subjects of animal study. Sailors lured
sharks to vessels with pieces of salt pork and
dissected them on deck where they thrilled to
the sight of baby sharks or swallowed fishes in
the animals' abdomens. Albatrosses were caught
to pose for written or graphic portraits, to provide
souvenir wings, and to furnish fresh meat for
supper.

Those journal keepers with artistic talent
drew almost anything that flew, floated, or swam
by. Illustrated logbooks and diaries contain portraits of everything from the smallest sea worm
to logs and spars afloat, to birds, seaweed, and
swordfish. Whalemen, who were expected to
note any spouting animal that they sighted or
caught, were skilled at depicting the leviathan
in various poses. One particularly anthropo-
morphic illustrator on the bark *Smyrna* in 1855
even gave his whales the ability to speak and
allowed each whale his vessel met to comment
upon the encounter. Whaling diarists who did
not have the talent or inclination for drawing
made decorative use of wooden whale stamps
and illustrated pages of their journals with criss-
crosses or patterns.

Despite the vast potential of the marine world

The

TUSKARIAN TIMES!

being a

JOURNAL *of* VOYAGE

FROM *Boston to Sumatra and Europe,*

IN THE

Commanded by Wm. C. Nutting.

from Oct 10th 1841 to Jan 15th 1843.

In honor of the retirement of his pea jacket, Isaac Baker composed an eight-stanza poem, which ended with the following verse:

> I'm growing old, I'm weak & rotten,
> It's time that I should be forgotten.—
> Farewell,—and may you never be
> Worn out, like your old Monkey pea.

Isaac Baker, *Tuskar*, 1841
Private Collection

Sharks, which sometimes followed vessels closely for several days at a time, were objects of intense curiosity and superstition among seamen. When a shark persisted in swimming close to a ship, sailors imagined that it was waiting for the death of a sailor so that it could feast upon the body. Some sailors decided to prey upon the shark before it preyed on them, and hooked salt pork onto lines to attract the shark in order to kill it.

Edward Haskell, *Tarquin*, 1862
Peabody Museum of Salem

Without the activity of towns, cities, or human society to distract them, sailors paid particular attention to natural phenomena. Here a comet is recognized as the most noteworthy event of March 12, 1843.

Anonymous, *LaFayette*, 1843
New Bedford Free Public Library

Left

Isaac Baker, *Tuskar,* 1841
Private Collection

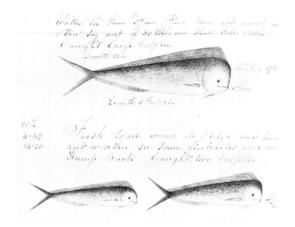

Not to be confused with the mammal of the same name, dolphin fish were regularly caught and eaten by sailors. The sight of a dying dolphin impressed those had never seen it before, because it turned every color of the rainbow as it expired.

Anonymous, *LaFayette*, 1843
New Bedford Free Public Library

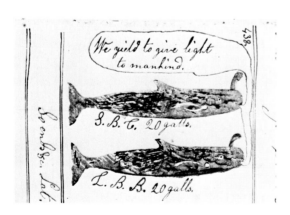

Whale stamp art was almost an independent genre, and its practitioners whittled wood into a variety of designs to signify the hunter and his prey. Even when a log keeper had seen or caught no whales, he devised signs for other events such as an anchor for making port, or a moon for lunar observations.

Henry Stinson, *Martha*, 1832
Kendall Whaling Museum

A particularly imaginative log keeper gave all of his whales the power of human speech. His sensitivity to the plight of whales may have compromised his ability to hunt, but it certainly enlivened his journal.

Anonymous, *Smyrna*, 1856
Nicholson Whaling Collection

Right

Whale stamps had a practical use—they made an easily visible record of a day's catch—but diarists recognized their aesthetic potential, and often used them as the means for non-representational designs. Here, one lone sperm whale is hidden in clusters of right whales.

Anonymous, *Lewis*, 1835–37
Kendall Whaling Museum

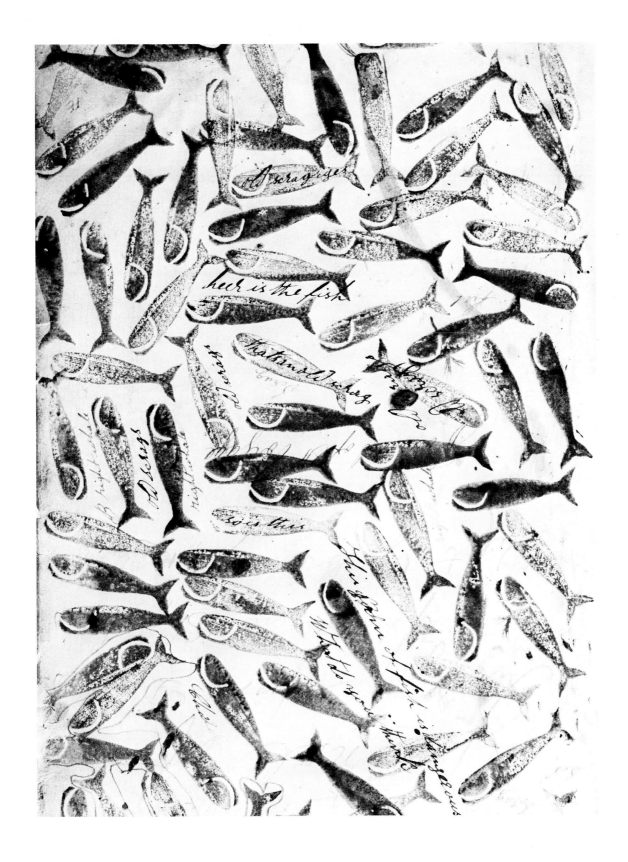

Anonymous, *LaFayette*, 1842
New Bedford Free Public Library

for journal keepers, nothing could compete with real crises for satisfying subject matter. Writers keenly anticipated possible wrecks, serious fights, or threatening storms. So eager were some of them for dramatic topics that events were occasionally rated according to their value as journal entries. On the bark *Sunbeam,* for instance, an incident occurred in 1869 that, although it never became a real emergency, was appreciated as if it had. As steward Silliman Ives noted on Tuesday, October 14, there was

Intense Excitement on board the Bark Sunbeam!! Anticipated attack upon the ship by Malay pirates!!! The decks cleared for action!!! Peaceful termination of the affair!

What had apparently happened aboard the *Sunbeam* was that as a group of whalemen had put off from the ship to catch some turtles they spotted native boats approaching them. Certain that they were under attack, the seamen made ready a rusty defense: one old six–pounder signal gun and six condemned muskets. But the pirates turned out to be friendly natives eager to trade. Even though the sailors were disappointed by the anticlimax, they were well-compensated, claimed Ives, by the boost the event gave to their diary keeping: ". . . So ends this days adventures. By and through them we have procured an item for our journals."

The sailors who used their diaries less as a record of observed events than as an outlet for their emotions had no difficulty completing regular entries. For them, diaries were a kind of intimate companion or confessor. In fact, when some of these men found themselves out of pen, ink, or paper, or at the end of a voyage, they experienced the loss of a valuable friend. Silliman Ives was so enamored of his journal that, at the end of his whaling voyage in 1871, he could barely say good-bye to his "faithful old log." Even as his anchor was being set in home port, Ives was busy making his last entries. The journal was, he claimed, a true "confidant."

Besides being supportive allies, journals provided some sailors with an opportunity to marvel at their own wit. Several seamen found the process of rereading their old entries endlessly fascinating. "I beleive I der[i]ve more pleasure from reading this old Journul than I would of bulwers greaitest work When I read this old Scriblings it put me in mind of old times . . ." wrote a nostalgic Edwin Pulver on the ship *Sea* in 1855. Likewise, William Abbe amused not only himself but his shipmates by reading portions of his diary aloud at night. "Been reading from my journal to the members of my watch," he wrote in 1859, "who to my delight—approve it—& Johnny the boatsteerer said he could keep awake all night listening to me & Curly tells me to have it printed when I get home."

Curly's suggestion to Abbe that he try to print his journal was probably not the first time the idea had crossed Abbe's mind. He was well aware of the successes of books like *Two Years Before The Mast* and may have intended to produce a similar publication. Even though most other diarists did not indicate plans to publish their works, they did expect that someone else,

Sailors could often tell where they were on the world's oceans by the types of birds that flew around them. Albatrosses, cape pigeons, and petrels provided welcome companionship to sailors working the difficult passages around Cape Horn and the Cape of Good Hope.

Isaac Baker, *John Caskie,* 1855
Private Collection

A few Cape Pigeons and Petrel around,

and "now and then" an

Albatross.

Anonymous, *Java*, 1860
New Bedford Free Public Library

William B. Haskell, *Marcella*, 1836
Nicholson Whaling Collection

at some time in the future, would read them. The self-consciousness of their writing shows that they expected their diaries to be seen by an outsider with a critical eye for spelling mistakes, grammatical errors, and poor penmanship, and they frequently felt the need to describe the difficulties under which they wrote. Augustus Hamblet on the bark *Hull,* for example, explained that it was not easy to write neatly on a rolling ship. "If any person should hereafter glance their eye over the first part of this Journal they will please excuse the bad Writing for the vessel is a knocking about so that it takes both hands and feet to hold on. . . ."

Likewise, Isaac Baker apologized for his errors on the fly leaf of the journal of the *Tuskar* in 1841:

Avast ye critics! throw off disguises
And on this page first turn your eyes
Ere you begin to criticize
The works of which I'm maker
Skip o'er each blot and each mistake
Each hasty line I'm forc'd to make
And other faults just for the sake
of that wild youth I . . . c Baker

Not all sailors felt compelled to apologize for their journals. Some were proud of their work, and were convinced of their diary's value as a guide to a foreign way of life. Several journal keepers even attempted to educate land-based readers by translating nautical terms like "duff" and "gam." For Horace Putnam on the *La Plata,* c. 1848, the trials of writing a journal were to be well-compensated if his readers learned something new: "Should there be a sentence interesting or fact new, unknown before, the object of it being written in part; will be accomplished and trouble repaid."

There was one sailor, at least, who did not look at his audiences with the charity of an ed-

John Martin, *Lucy Ann*, c. 1841
Kendall Whaling Museum

This was Baker's last journal. He died halfway through the voyage—hence the incomplete termination date.

Isaac Baker, *Tarquin*, 1862
Private Collection

ucator. Ambrose Bates was more interested in what his future readers offered him than in how he might serve them. For Bates, the fact that his journal might one day be read was his key to a kind of immortality. Even if he died at sea, in an unmarked grave, at least his diary would give those he loved a way to remember him. As he wrote in 1867: ". . . if it be my lot to leave this form of clay upon some corral bed. Or upon the desolate shore of a frozen zone. I shall not go unmourned for I believe there are those who would miss me many a long day. And perhaps this book may reach them and these unworthy museings of mine may cheer their remembrance of me."

But Bates wanted to be remembered even beyond the generation in which he lived. He explained in a journal to his wife in 1868: "The future looks dark and dreary My life o how weary But time rules on and unless Annie you and me shall live in a future world to tell the sadness of our seperation and the joyes of our meetings yes unless all these, one thousand years from now no tongue can tell our names our loves or that we ever were."

By the simple act of journal keeping and through the lucky circumstances that preserved his diaries to the present day, Ambrose Bates has found a modest immortality. Like the one hundred and three other sailors whose writings inform this account, his name and the fact of his life have not been lost.

List of Journal Keepers

Journal Keepers	Vessel(s)	Dates of Journal*	By Permission of:
William A. Abbe	*Atkins Adams*	1858–59	Whaling Museum Library of the Old Dartmouth Historical Society
John F. Aiken	*Virginia*	1843–47	The Kendall Whaling Museum
James Allen	*Alfred Gibbs*	1870–73	Nicholson Whaling Collection in the Providence Public Library
Samuel Allen	*William Wirt*	1846–50	Peabody Museum of Salem
Anonymous	*Brunette*	1842–43	Nicholson Whaling Collection in the Providence Public Library
Anonymous	*Sarah*	1847	Peabody Museum of Salem
Anonymous	*Stephen Glover*	1863–64	Peabody Museum of Salem
Anonymous	*Zone*	1855–58	The Kendall Whaling Museum
Anonymous	*Elizabeth*	1847–51	Peabody Museum of Salem
Charles G. Arthur	*James Maury*	1841–45	The Kendall Whaling Museum
Charles Austin	*Charles Phelps*	1842–44	Whaling Museum Library of the Old Dartmouth Historical Society
G.S.B.	*George*	1839–40	Mystic Seaport Museum
Isaac Baker	*Warsaw*	1840–41	Katharine Baker Kellom
	Tuskar	1841–42	
	John Caskie	1855–56	
	Merrimac	1858	
	Tarquin	1862	
Charles F. Barnard	*Resolute*	1858–59	Mystic Seaport Museum
Ambrose Bates	*Euphrates, Nimrod,*	1860–61	The Kendall Whaling Museum
	Milwood, Isabella	1867–68	
John Battis	*Arctic*	1864–65	Essex Institute
John Beebe	*Peru*	185–	Nantucket Historical Association
Charles A. Benson	*Glide*	1862	Essex Institute
		1864	
		1878–79	
		1880	
James Bond	*John Parker*	1852–54	New Bedford Free Public Library
Benjamin Boodry	*Arnolda*	1852–53	Whaling Museum Library of the Old Dartmouth Historical Society
	Fanny	1856–57	
George L. Bowman	*Addison*	1859–60	Nicholson Whaling Collection in the Providence Public Library
	Albion	1867–70	
	Europa	1870–71	
Richard Boyenton	*Bengal*	1833–35	Essex Institute
Samuel T. Braley	*Arab*	1849–52	The Kendall Whaling Museum
Abram Briggs	*Eliza Adams*	1872–76	Whaling Museum Library of the Old Dartmouth Historical Society
Thomas R. Bryant	*Elizabeth*	1847–51	The Kendall Whaling Museum
F. Cady	*Julian*	1847–50	The Kendall Whaling Museum
James H. Cather	*Roman*	1854–55	The Kendall Whaling Museum

* Date of journal does not necessarily correspond with date of ship's voyage.

Journal Keepers	Vessel(s)	Dates of Journal	By Permission of:
John H. Chapman	*Monsoon*	1857–59	Mystic Seaport Museum
John Cleland, Jr.	*Ceres*	1835–37	The Mariners' Museum
John Crimblish	*Palestine*	1839–42	Essex Institute
Stephen Curtis	*Mercury*	1841–44	New Bedford Free Public Library
Henry L. Davis	*South America*	1862–63	Mystic Seaport Museum
Solomon Davis	*Mindoro*	1845–46	Essex Institute
Joseph Dias	*Pocohontas*	1850–53	Whaling Museum Library of the Old Dartmouth
	St. George	1853–55	Historical Society
John Eagleston	*Mermaid*	1836–39	Essex Institute
	Troy	1860–62	
Charles Emery	*Columbus*	1839	Peabody Museum of Salem
Silas Fitch	*Charles Phelps*	1842–44	Mystic Seaport Museum
Washington Fosdick	*Emeline*	1843–44	Whaling Museum Library of the Old Dartmouth
	Montreal	1851–52	Historical Society
George Gardner	*Nantucket*	1841–45	Nantucket Historical Association
Ezra Goodnough	*Ann Perry*	1845–47	Peabody Museum of Salem
Henry Green	*Hudson*	1835–39	Mystic Seaport Museum
E.F.H.	*Sumatra*	1868–71	Essex Institute
Augustus Hamblet	*Hull*	1838–39	Peabody Museum of Salem
	St. Paul	1839–40	
Edward Harrington	*Oregon*	1840	Essex Institute
Edward Haskell	*Tarquin*	1862–63	Peabody Museum of Salem
J. E. Haviland	*Baltic*	1856–58	Nicholson Whaling Collection in the Providence Public Library
J. Hersey	*Esquimaux*	1843	The Kendall Whaling Museum
Richard W. Hixson	*Maria*	1832–36	The Houghton Library, Harvard University
Caleb F. Hunt	*S.R. Roper*	1865–66	The Kendall Whaling Museum
Silliman Ives (Murphy McGuire, pseudonym)	*Sunbeam*	1868–71	Whaling Museum Library of the Old Dartmouth Historical Society
Edward N. Jenney	*Alfred Gibbs*	1859–63	Whaling Museum Library of the Old Dartmouth Historical Society
Edmund Jennings	*Alfred Gibbs*	1865–69	Nicholson Whaling Collection in the Providence Public Library
Henry M. Johnson	*Acushnet*	1845–47	Peabody Museum of Salem
John Jones	*Eliza Adams*	1852–54	The Kendall Whaling Museum
John Joplin	*Ann Perry*	1847–48	Peabody Museum of Salem
Marshall Keith	*Brewster*	1863–64	Nicholson Whaling Collection in the Providence Public Library
	Cape Horn Pigeon	1866–69	Whaling Museum Library of the Old Dartmouth Historical Society
Edward J. Kirwin	*William Gifford*	1871–72	The Kendall Whaling Museum
James O. Knapp	*Merrimac*	1854–55	Mystic Seaport Museum
John Land	*Splendid*	1842–43	Mystic Seaport Museum
Henry Lascomb	*Elizabeth*	1844–48	Peabody Museum of Salem
Beriah Manchester	*Persia*	1846–49	Whaling Museum Library of the Old Dartmouth Historical Society
John Martin	*Lucy Ann*	1841–44	The Kendall Whaling Museum
W. L. Maxfeld	*Niger*	1852–56	The Houghton Library, Harvard University
William Maxfield	*Pioneer*	1869–72	Whaling Museum Library of the Old Dartmouth Historical Society

Journal Keepers	Vessel(s)	Dates of Journal	By Permission of:
George E. Mills	*Leonidas*	1856	The Kendall Whaling Museum
Edward Mitchell	*Ivanhoe*	1866–67	Penobscot Marine Museum
Harry B. Mitchell	*Fairy*	1861–63	Mystic Seaport Museum
Francis A. Moreland	*Sooloo*	1861–62	Peabody Museum of Salem
Thomas Morrison	*Active*	1852–54	Nicholson Whaling Collection in the Providence Public Library
Thomas Morrison	*Avola*	1870–74 1874–77	The Kendall Whaling Museum
Benjamin Neal	*Reaper*	1837–39	Essex Institute
Allen W. Newman	*Covington*	1852–54 1856–59	Nicholson Whaling Collection in the Providence Public Library
Avery F. Parker	*Midas*	1842–44	Whaling Museum Library of the Old Dartmouth Historical Society
George Parker	*Orray Taft*	1866–67	The Kendall Whaling Museum
James H. Payne	*Franklin* *Rambler* *Monticello*	1853–55 1855 1856–58	Nicholson Whaling Collection in the Providence Public Library
William B. Peacock	*Congress*	1857–59	The Kendall Whaling Museum
Clothier Pierce	*Rodman* *Minnesota*	1855–59 1868–73	Whaling Museum Library of the Old Dartmouth Historical Society
G. P. Pomeroy	*Adeline Gibbs*	1853–56	Mystic Seaport Museum
Edwin C. Pulver	*Columbus* *Sea*	1851–52 1852–55	Nicholson Whaling Collection in the Providence Public Library
Horace Putnam	*William Schroder* *Cherokee,* *La Plata* *Emily Wilder*	184– 184– 185–	Essex Institute
John Randall	*California*	1849–51	Whaling Museum Library of the Old Dartmouth Historical Society
John Randall	*Cleora*	1852–55	Whaling Museum Library of the Old Dartmouth Historical Society
Joseph E. Ray	*Edward Cary*	1854–58	Nantucket Historical Association
Nathaniel G. Robinson	*Nantasket*	1843	Peabody Museum of Salem
George Russell	*Bengal*	1832–33	Essex Institute
Orson Shattuck (Charles Perkins, pseudonym)	*Frances* *Eliza Mason*	1850–52 1853–56	Whaling Museum Library of the Old Dartmouth Historical Society
John Spooner	*Mt. Wollaston*	1861–64	New Bedford Free Public Library
John A. States	*Nantasket* *William Wirt*	1845–46 1846	Mystic Seaport Museum
Charles Stedman	*Mt. Wollaston*	1853–54	New Bedford Free Public Library
William Stetson	*Arab*	1853–57	Whaling Museum Library of the Old Dartmouth Historical Society
J. R. Stivers	*Eliza Adams*	1872–76	Whaling Museum Library of the Old Dartmouth Historical Society
Sylvanus C. Tallman	*Canada*	1846–49	Whaling Museum Library of the Old Dartmouth Historical Society
William C. Taylor	*Angelia*	1861–62	Essex Institute
William W. Taylor	*South Carolina*	1835–37	The Kendall Whaling Museum
William H. Townsend	*Imaum*	1858–59	Mystic Seaport Museum

Journal Keepers	Vessel(s)	Dates of Journal	By Permission of:
Elias Trotter	*Illinois*	1845–47	Whaling Museum Library of the Old Dartmouth Historical Society
Ambrose Waldron	*Bowditch*	1846–49 1852–54	Nicholson Whaling Collection in the Providence Public Library
D. F. Weekes	*Brothers*	1866	Peabody Museum of Salem
Robert Weir	*Clara Bell*	1855–58	Mystic Seaport Museum
Dan Whitfield	*Doctor Franklin*	1856	Barbara Johnson Collection
Holden N. Willcox	*Columbus*	1837–39	The Kendall Whaling Museum
William H. Wilson	*Cavalier*	1848–50	Mystic Seaport Museum
Samuel P. Winegar	*Julian*	1858–60	David Wagstaff Collection, Yale University Library
Joseph Winn	*Heraclide*	1835	Essex Institute

List of Illustrators

Illustrator	Vessel(s)	Dates of Manuscript	By Permission of:
Anonymous	*Java*	1860–63	New Bedford Free Public Library
Anonymous	*LaFayette*	1840–44	New Bedford Free Public Library
Anonymous	*Lewis*	1835–37	The Kendall Whaling Museum
Anonymous	*Orray Taft*	c. 1864	The Kendall Whaling Museum
Anonymous	*Sea Ranger*	n.d.	The Kendall Whaling Museum
Anonymous	*Sketchbook A-135*	n.d.	The Kendall Whaling Museum
Anonymous	*Smyrna*	1853–56	Nicholson Whaling Collection in the Providence Public Library
Isaac Baker	*Warsaw*	1840–41	Katharine Baker Kellom
	Tuskar	1841–42	
	John Caskie	1855–56	
	Merrimac	1858	
	Golconda	1859	
	Tarquin	1862	
Washington Fosdick	*Emeline*	1843–44	Whaling Museum Library of the Old Dartmouth Historical Society
Abraham Gardner?	*Canton*	1834–38	The Kendall Whaling Museum
Andrew Haraden	*George*	1831–32	Peabody Museum of Salem
Edward Haskell	*Tarquin*	1862–63	Peabody Museum of Salem
William B. Haskell	*Marcella*	1836–41	Nicholson Whaling Collection in the Providence Public Library
Henry M. Johnson	*Acushnet*	1845–47	Peabody Museum of Salem
Peleg Lawrence	*Elizabeth*	1849	Peabody Museum of Salem
John Martin	*Lucy Ann*	1841–44	The Kendall Whaling Museum
Joseph Ray	*Edward Cary*	1854–58	Nantucket Historical Association
James Skinner? (in log of *Morning Star*)	*Concordia*	1867 1864–65	Nicholson Whaling Collection in the Providence Public Library
Frederick H. Smith	*Petrel*	1871–74	The Kendall Whaling Museum
George Soule	*St. George*	1865–69	Nicholson Whaling Collection in the Providence Public Library
Henry Stinson	*Martha*	1829–33	The Kendall Whaling Museum
William C. Taylor	*Angelia*	1861–62	Essex Institute
Henry Tuttle	*LaGrange*	1849	Essex Institute
Robert Weir	*Clara Bell*	1855–58	Mystic Seaport Museum

Catalogue of Objects

p. 2 Oilskin pants

Oiled cotton waterproof pants, overall length 101 cm, M-5673.

p. 5 Tarred hat

Sailor's hat of straw covered with tarred canvas, ca. late 1800s, width at widest point 33 cm, M-995.

p. 6 Sea chest with belongings

Slant–sided painted pine sea chest with leather–covered rope beckets and hand–made strap hinges, ca. 1850, base 108×50 cm, height 51 cm, M-3540.

Front, l. to r.: canvas ditty bag with string handles, length 36 cm, M-5179; painted wooden mirror with silvered glass, tongue and groove fitted lid painted with a decorative design and the name "Joseph Archer," length 28 cm, M-492; twist of tobacco, length 15 cm, M-2799; clay pipe covered with macrame with engraved metal band and horn bit, length 15 cm, M-7155; knife in leather sheath, length 27 cm, M-5658.

Second row, l. to r.: sailor's hat (see above); journal kept on board the *Tarquin*, 1862–3, by Edward Haskell, height 17 cm, Phillips Library 656-1863T; testament with sewn canvas cover initialled "A.H.W.", length 18.5 cm, Phillips Library, 1647.4/B582/1784; ditty box containing sewing bag (M-9837), diameter 19 cm, M-3476; pewter plate marked "I. Trask," diameter 21 cm, M-18112; pewter beaker marked "O. Trask," height 8 cm, M-18111.

In sea chest: leather belt with brass buckle and stud, length 138 cm, M-1419; oiled cotton pants (see above); *New-York Daily Tribune*, Tuesday, February 11, 1857, Phillips Library; Nautilus shell, white with brown markings, width 18 cm, Natural History Collection; letters, Phillips Library; daguerrotype of Charles Edwin and Susan Augusta Ballard in case with design, faced with velvet marked "Wᵐ Snell, Artist, Salem," height 12 cm, M-14519; cloth breeches, overall length 104 cm, M-6537; dried sea horse, length 12.5 cm, Natural History Collection.

p. 14 Hard tack

Hard biscuit, ca. 1800, diameter 10 cm, M-3500.

p. 16 Medicine chest

Medicine chest made and used by Jonathan P. Saunders on his voyages ca. 1837, painted wood with brass bale handles. Compartmented, with glass bottles and packets of medicine, length 51 cm, M-1342.

p. 17 Surgeon's kit

Brass–bound mahogany case containing surgical instruments and dental equipment, ca. 1820–30, width 51 cm, M-14214.

p. 20 Mail bag

Cotton letter bag with drawstring top, stencilled "CERES," length 78.5 cm, M-3101.

p. 24 Whaling instruments

19th–century whaling instruments: lance, length 262 cm, M-1768; two-flued harpoon, length 254 cm, M-912; single-flued harpoon, length 243.5 cm, M-4307; toggle harpoon, length 247 cm, M-915; toggle harpoon, length 234.5 cm, M-1725; cutting spade, length 250 cm, M-19083; porpoise fork, length 220.5, M-1625; blubber pick, length 219 cm, M-1540; blubber fork, length 183.5 cm, M-1609.

p. 24 Twisted harpoon

Harpoon head of wrought iron, length (twisted) 34.5 cm, M-914.

p. 33 Traverse board

Maple, circular board incised with points painted alternately red and blue, with speed table below, 19th century, height 40 cm, M-1427.

p. 34 Sailmaker's bag

Canvas bag with knotted handles, overall length 80 cm, M-3764.

Wooden fid, length 39 cm, M-3764; wooden fid, length 21.5 cm, M-3764; wooden thimble, diameter 5.5 cm, M-3764; wooden seam rubber, length 11 cm, M-1149; leather palm with raised indented metal section, width 11 cm, M-19077; horn grease cup, height 8.5 cm, M-3764; wooden–handled awl, length 12.5 cm, M-3764; wooden needle case, length 13.5 cm, M-2990; sail needles in wooden needle case covered with macrame, length 15 cm, M-19078.

p. 38 Leg and wrist irons

Sliding leg irons with toggle fastening, length 38 cm, M-1071; iron handcuffs with key, width 10 cm, key length 8.5 cm, M-1427; leg irons on chain, overall length 68 cm, M-973.

p. 38 Brass knuckles and sling shot

Brass knuckles, width 10 cm, M-10949; weighted weapon made of twine-covered shot with a noose at one end, length 50 cm, M-911.

p. 38 Colt revolver

.36 caliber pistol, old model Navy (1851 model), cylinder engraved with Naval battle, length 33 cm, M-2458.

p. 49 Initiation implements

Oversized wooden razor, with blade painted silver, length unopened 33 cm, M-9692; painted wooden bucket with whalebone handle, marked "BARK LANCER," height with handle, 46 cm, M-1614; brass speaking trumpet, height 56 cm, M-1549; porpoise fork, length 220.5 cm, M-1625.

p. 54 Accordion

Soft wood box with inlaid decoration of brass with celluloid (?), leather bellows gilded with painted silver foil, brass and pearl shell keys, ca. 1850s, width 38 cm, M-1930.

p. 55 Scrimshaw tooth and book

Scrimshawed whale tooth, height 17 cm, M-18988; *Fanny Campbell, The Female Pirate*, by "Lieutenant Murray," Phillips Library, 1085/B193/1845, height 26 cm.

p. 56 Model in bottle

Model of saw and trestle in seamed bottle with carved wood stopper, height 29 cm, M-1414.

p. 57   Beckets

Pair of ropework beckets with painted tack knots, height 27 cm, M-10698.

p. 66   Souvenirs from China

Cricket cage, gourd with relief surface scene of several people, perhaps with clear lacquer, with rose wood pierced top, length 12 cm, E-56214; ivory jackstraws in paper box, box length 9 cm, E-3296; wood tea caddy with black lacquer and gold lacquer designs of garden and river scenes (originally contained pewter tea boxes), width 20 cm, E-28942; silk panels with silk thread embroidery, length 78.5 cm, E-61758.

p. 66   Human hair necklace

Hawaiian necklace of braided human hair with walrus ivory hook and cord of olona fiber, mid to late 19th century, 42 cm, E-41001.

p. 66   Fijian eating fork

Carved wooden fork with five tines, mid to late 19th century, length 20 cm, E-28705.

p. 66   Parrot in whalebone cage

African Gray parrot (*Psittacus Erithacus*), height 30.5 cm, M-1619A, in dome-topped panbone cage pegged with bone and metal nails, height 53 cm, M-1619.

Color illustration   Sailor's valentine

Octagonal hinged wooden case with glass covers and decoration of pastel–shaded mollusc shells, width 30.5 cm, courtesy of Mr. and Mrs. Robert Storer.

Illustrations

All the illustrations featured in *Dogwatch and Liberty Days* are, as far as can be determined, the products of working deepwater sailors in the nineteenth century. All but two (the anonymous sketchbook and the *Sea Ranger* sketchbook) are contained in sailors' journals. All of the illustrations are 30×22 cm or smaller, and are executed in pen and ink, pencil, wash, or watercolor.

Index

Abbe, William, 9, 12, 18, 21, 26, 28, 45, 53, 59, 67, 74
Africa, 61
Aftercabin, see Officers
Afterguard, see Officers
Aiken, John F., 64
Albany, NY, 45
Alcohol, see Liquor
Allen, James, 17, 69
America, 1–2, 19, 20, 23; East Coast, 45
Anonymous, *Concordia*, 19
Anonymous, *Java*, 76
Anonymous, *Lafayette*, 71, 72
Anonymous, *Lewis*, 73
Anonymous, *Orray Taft*, 25, 27, 41, 43, 62; color illustrations
Anonymous, *Sea Ranger*, 62, 64
Anonymous Sketchbook, 5, 22
Anonymous, *Smyrna*, 72
Anxiety, 9, 10–12
Arctic Ocean, 1, 10–11
Articles, Shipping: signing of, 35–6
    power of, 44
    why signed, 45–6
Ascension Island, 68
Atkins Adams, (William Abbe), 35
Atlantic Ocean, 11
Austin, Charles, 48
Authority, see Consuls, Captain, Discipline, Federal Regulations, Officers, Power, Shipping Articles

Baker, Isaac, 10, 15, 18, 30–31, 34, 47, 49, 50, 52, 54, 57, 69, 70, 71, 74, 76, 77
Barbados, color illustration
Barnard, Charles, 20
Bates, Ambrose, 9, 39, 46, 60, 77
Battis, John, 9–10
Bay of Islands, New Zealand, 62
Beachcombers, 67–8
Beckets, on sea chest, 7, 57
Benson, Charles A., 11, 20, 45
Birds, sea, 75
Boatsteerers, 1, 53, 57
Boodry, Benjamin, 56
Boston, 9, 30, 38, 48
Boyenton, Richard, 2, 21
Braley, Samuel T., 10, 20, 22, 40
Brass knuckles, 38
Brazil, 34
Briggs, Abram, 45
Bryant, Thomas R., 49

Cady, F., 68
Calcutta, 38
Canton, 67
Cape Cod, 42
Cape Horn, 12, 53
Captain: and crew lists, 2
    reputation, 30, 34, 40–44

shipboard authority, 35–6
fairness of judgment, 39
and sick sailors, 40
in port, 40, 42
on endangered vessel, 42
and home port, 40, 42
and Neptune Ceremony, 49–51
social life, 65
Celebes, 65
Chile, 42
China, 67
Cleanliness, on board ship, 16–17
Cleland, John Jr., 12, 42, 44
Clothing, 2, 5, 71
Colt, 38
Columbus, (Charles Emery), 23
Comet, 71
Congress, (William B. Peacock), 9
Consul: as arbitrator, 39
    formal protest to, 42
    authority behind captain, 44
    visiting, in port, 65
Cook, Captain, burial place, 65
Cook, ship's, 1, 35, 49
Crafts, on board ship, 56–7
Crews: size of, 28
    race of, 35
    full crews, 45
    changing, in port, 65
    See also: Desertion, Discharge, Greenhands, Hierarchy, Shanghaiing
Crew lists: 1–2
    falsifying of, 2
Curfew, during liberty days, 64
Curtis, Stephen, 35

Daguerreotypes, 7, 57
Dancing, 1, 18, 53, 58, 59, 61
Davidson, Thomas, cover illustration
Davis, Henry L., 42, 58
Death, 10–11, 55–6, 77
Desertion: 28, 65–8
    an imprisonable offence, 36
    prescribed punishments for, 39
    to avoid reprisals, 42
Dias, Joseph, 44
Discharge, 9, 42, 65
Discipline, 35–8. See also Captain, Flogging, Irons, Power
Dogwatch: 1, 18
    relaxation during second dogwatch, 52–9
Dolphin fish, 72
Drifters, 67–8
Drunkenness: old hands, 1
    and temperance vessels, 36
    and dereliction of duty, 39
    unpunished, 42
    going to sea a cure for, 45–6
    shipping of drunk men, 45
    during liberty days, 60–1

East Indies, 14, 48
Edgartown, 42
Elitism, of seamen, 4, 48, 50
Ellis, Captain Benjamin, 87
Equator, 48
Europe, 1

Family life: anxiety about, 20
    news of in letters, 20
    missing, 39

restless despite, 46
    families in foreign ports, 61–2
    journal kept for family, 77
Federal regulations, 35–6
Fighting: among sailors, 35, 41
    between watches, 35
    during Neptune Ceremony, 49–50
Fiji, 67
Flogging, 36–7, 39
Food, on board ship: 12–13, 69
    monotony of, 9
    hard tack, 14
    livestock on board, 14
    cause of friction, 35
    fresh food in port, 60, 64
Forecastle, 1, 52
Fosdick, Washington, 46, 53
Freedom, individual, of foremast hands:
    and shipping articles, 35
    restricted, as punishment, 39
    and Neptune Ceremony, 50
Friction, on board ship: 35–6
    and Neptune Ceremony, 49–50
Frustration, affecting judgment, 39. See also Tedium, Isolation, Anxiety

Gamming, 19, 57–9
Gardner, Abraham (?), color illustration
Gardner, George, 44
Goodnough, Ezra, 19, 61
Greenhands: 9
    and Neptune Ceremony, 48–51
Grenadine, color illustration

Hamblet, Augustus, 76
Haraden, Andrew, 8, 31
Harbormaster, 64
Hard tack, 14
Hardships, of seafaring life: 1, 9–20
    attraction of, 45–6
    See also, Food, Hazards, Health, Sleep
Harrington, Edward, 69
Haskell, Captain Dennis, 35
Haskell, Edward, 2, 8, 11, 12, 29, 30, 48–51, 58, 68, 71; color illustration
Haskell, William, 76; color illustration
Hat, tarred, 5
Haviland, J. E., 16, 40, 59, 64, 68
Hazards, of seafaring life: 4–5, 10–11, 16–17, 24–5, 28, 39
    attractions of, 46–7
    as subject matter for journals, 74
Health: seasickness, 9
    infections, 10
    and malnutrition, 16
    medicine chest, 16
    surgeon's kit, 17
    feigning illness, 40
    going to sea to improve, 45
    and liberty days, 68
    venereal diseases, 68
Heath, Captain William, 39
Hersey, J., 53
Hierarchy, social, of deepwater sailors, 1, 9, 22, 57
Holidays, American, 54
Home port: of 104 journal keepers, 1
    anxiety as approaching, 20
    gossip in, 42
    end of voyage, 74
    See also Family life, Letters, Newspapers
Hong Kong, 67